Beshert

Beshert

✦

True Stories of Connections

Harry Samuels

Foreword by
Rabbi Micah D. Greenstein

iUniverse, Inc.
New York Lincoln Shanghai

Beshert
True Stories of Connections

iUniverse, Inc.

For information address:
iUniverse, Inc.
2021 Pine Lake Road, Suite 100
Lincoln, NE 68512
www.iuniverse.com

ISBN: 0-595-31437-6

Printed in the United States of America

To David Alan Samuels (1968–1988)
Of Blessed Memory
And To My Soul Mate, Best Friend, and *Beshert*,
Flora Samuels

There are more things in heaven and earth, Horatio, than are dreamt of in your philosophy.

—William Shakespeare

Contents

ACKNOWLEGMENTS

I am deeply indebted to Mrs. Arthur (Jane) Lettes for extending her editing expertise to a first-time author. She has not only been of invaluable help in polishing this manuscript, but in the process, she has become a friend.

He came Fridays, often with his daughter, to sing psalms to her and to comfort the dying old lady at the Memphis Jewish Home. He told her, "If you can't come to services, services will come to you." The Memphis community is blessed to have Rabbi Micah Greenstein. His immediate acceptance of the request for a *Foreword* was very touching and greatly appreciated.

Thank you seems inadequate for Dr. Stephen Tabachnick, matchmaker and advisor, who was always available to provide enthusiasm and expertise.

Gilbert Halpern and Rabbi Levi Klein have been of enormous assistance to one who is computer challenged.

To the following, who contributed these stories and valuable recommendations, go my profound thanks and gratitude: Dr. Edward Berg, Maris Frager Berg, Bert Bornblum, Rabbi Moshe Bryski, Dr. Albert and Deanna Burson, Gene Camerik, Joel Felt, Dr. Stanley Frager, Bernard Freiden, Theo Garb, Martin and Ruth Geller, Jeffery Gerecke, Oscar Goldberg, E. J. Goldsmith, Jr., Alvin and Elaine Gordon, Marlin Graber, Rabbi Efraim Greenblatt, Murray Habbaz, Beverly Halpern, Dr. Aryeh and Tamar Kasher, Henry W. Kimmel, George W. King, Bernard Kivowitz, Rabbi Levi Klein, Menachem Klein, Marjean Kremer, Rabbi Benjamin Levene, Tricia Lewis, Jerome Makowsky, May Lynn Mansbach, Lynnie Mirvis, Tova Mirvis, Harold and Ronna Newburger, Heidi Newman, Leonard and Louise Newman, Lyda Parker, Naava Parker, Dr. David Patterson, Philip Pliner, Sydney and Marilyn Pollack, Scott and Shay Poole, Stephen Posner, Dr. Bryan Rigg, Leonid and Friderica Saharovici, Flora Samuels, Sherri Samuels, Dr. Donald and Harriett Schaffer, Dr. Pierre Secher, Judy Sheon, Dr. Robert and Irma Sheon, Malky Shine, Victor Shine, Shelley Smuckler, Charles Steinberg, and Mike Stoller.

If anyone wishes to provide a story for a subsequent publication, I will be pleased to give it proper attribution and to extend my sincere and profound thanks. Please address all correspondence to Harry Samuels, P.O. Box 17456, Memphis,

Tennessee 38187-0456, or to my e-mail address: BeshertStories@aol.com. All proceeds received by the author will be donated to the David Alan Samuels Charitable Fund.

Harry Samuels

FOREWORD

Rabbi Micah D. Greenstein

Each of us owes our life to people we have never known. Had it not been for a rabbi in Ithica, New York, my parents would not have met and I would never have been born. Certainly, there are invisible lines of connection which link human beings, places, and moments in uncanny and meaningful ways. Harry Samuels' *Beshert: True Stories of Connections* is a tribute to that idea.

We all know that our loved ones live on in the acts of goodness they performed and in the hearts of those who cherish their memory. Is it possible that deceased loved ones continue to guide us in the here and now? Harry Samuels suggests that possibility, too, in homage to his beloved son, David Alan Samuels, who died in 1988 at age nineteen.

The author employs the Jungian definition of "synchronicity" to explain the book's Yiddish title, "*Beshert.*" *Synchronicity* "is the meaningful coincidence of two or more events where probability or chance is not involved." It implies purpose rather than randomness.

Among the seventy-seven stories in this enjoyable volume are the stories of a life-saving phone number left on a matchbook in Nazi Europe; discovering close connections with total strangers halfway around the world while cruising on the high seas; just missed airplane crashes; and miracle workers who appear out of nowhere.

One of my teachers, Rabbi Lawrence Kushner, teaches that our lives are not from G-d or by G-d. They are *of* God. "There is only one player: God." In the words of Deuteronomy 6:4, "The Lord alone is G-d: There is nothing else!" "Everything, therefore, exists and derives its reality from G-d, *including us.*" "When we raise our consciousness," Kushner writes, "we not only realize that we have never really been apart from our divine Source at all, we realize that we also participate in the process itself."

As I read the rather amazing stories Harry Samuels has written and culled from various writers as well as from his own experiences, the collection raised more questions than answers. For instance, an individual like George King who survived Pan Am Flight 103 by postponing his flight to witness a sunrise in Israel cannot help but see his escape from danger as miraculous. Were the other ticket purchasers on Pan Am Flight 103, including a congregant of mine, meant to die, while Mr. King was meant to live? Harry Samuels doesn't make that assertion any more than he argues that his own son was meant to die.

What is evident from these stories, though, is a truth we too often forget. While we are not always the recipients of the blessings we share nor are we always the ones who suffer immediately from our misdeeds, when we do carry out our good deeds, we can be sure that someone else in the universe will be the beneficiary of our actions and that that someone else is often closer to us than we realize. If nothing else, the personal accounts in Samuels' *Beshert* suggest how randomness can give way to acknowledgment of the Source from Whom every story and every life flow.

As I read about angels appearing in the form of other people and how prayers for healing resulted in prayers "answered," dozens more examples from my own rabbinic experience came to mind. While readers will be stirred to think of their own *beshert* life stories, they will be equally inspired by the response of the individuals in this volume, the common selfless reaction to the miraculous experience each underwent. I was as moved by Harry Samuels' commentary on what these individuals have done for others as a result of their wake-up calls as I was by the stories themselves.

Enjoy this book. It's hard not to.

INTRODUCTION

Harry Samuels

Beshert is a Yiddish word meaning divine providence, fate, destiny or inevitability. Sometimes it refers to finding a life partner or a soul mate. But in all instances, it implies purpose. *Beshert* describes things meant to be, never chance occurrences.

Most of us have experienced, or have known, of events that were not likely to have happened. Had we considered the circumstances, we might have attributed such events to serendipity or coincidence or synchronicity. Serendipity is considered pure chance. It is a lucky break, a fortunate find, a happy discovery. It is being in the right place at the right time.

Coincidence is somewhat chaotic in nature. It describes accidental and remarkable events or ideas that appear to be connected to each other but lack a causal relationship. To some of us, there is no such thing as coincidence. A friend feels that "coincidence is G-d's way of remaining anonymous."

"Synchronicity," according to Carl Jung, "is the *meaningful* coincidence of two or more events where probability or chance is not involved." It implies purpose rather than randomness, and it is this concept that best describes the incidents included in this book.

The following anecdotes about synchronicity include accounts of people finding connections with each other in unexpected places and under unforeseeable circumstances. In some cases, the connections significantly altered, or even saved, the participants' lives. These stories are offered not to burden the reader with philosophical discourse but to allow each to reach his or her own conclusion about their meaning. Many who have heard or read these stories have acknowledged similar experiences in their own lives.

It is my belief that there is purpose in life and a reason for everything that happens. In this sense everything is connected. I believe as well that we seldom understand the reasons behind our involvement in an event. Often we must distance ourselves from an incident before we gain the perspective to understand it—and even then we may grasp only a portion of the meaning. I think of life as a divine symphony, with much harmony we call happiness and much dissonance we call pain and suffering, all under the direction of the Composer who is the only one who knows the entire score.

Many of us are aware that the consequences of our actions can extend far beyond what we originally intended. Stephen J. Dubner, in his book *Turbulent Souls*, writes, "Only when a good piece of your life has unspooled can you look back and see how one connection led to the next, how a seemingly random sequence of events conspired to propel you down a certain path, and then you begin to doubt that there was anything random about your journey at all."

The impetus for much of what my wife and I have tried to achieve stems from the devastating death in 1988 of our then nineteen-year-old son, David Alan Samuels. The only response to his death that made sense to us was to enhance life. We began to devote more and more of our time to developing and expanding various social services that we knew our compassionate son would have supported. In a high school English paper entitled "Future Plans" that he composed at age sixteen, David wrote, "The final goal of my life will be to repay society with what I can offer for what it has given me. There is a story in the *Talmud* that tells of an old man planting a carob tree that takes seventy years to bear fruit. Someone asked, 'Why plant this tree when you cannot enjoy its fruit?' He replied, 'Others have done for me and I am doing for the next generation.'" Motivated by that spirit, we were encouraged to reach out to others, enabling us to make connections with a wide range of individuals, often in unexpected places and with fortuitous results. Some of the stories that follow are drawn from people we met while making those efforts.

PART I
OF LIFE AND DEATH

THE FLYING LESSON

Harry Samuels

In 1956 my cousin Victor Shainberg and I purchased a store in Jonesboro, Arkansas, and established a wonderful partnership that lasted until his death in 1986. We were in our early twenties when we moved to Jonesboro, far away from all vestiges of parental control, and at our first opportunity, we began taking flying lessons.

On a beautiful Sunday morning in 1957, I tried unsuccessfully to convince myself to get out of bed in order to take a flying lesson scheduled for 9:00 A.M. The previous night had been a full one for both Victor and me. We had spent a busy day at our store and then had gone to a late party. The prospect of only a few hours' sleep was not appealing. Victor had already left for his lesson at 8:00 A.M., and mine was scheduled next. I called the airport, and the instructor agreed to take another student in my time slot and to reschedule me for 10:00 A.M.

At approximately 9:45 A.M., a man from Paragould, Arkansas, flew his low-winged Beechcraft Bonanza airplane over the Jonesboro airport just as my replacement and his instructor were flying their high-winged Cessna below him. The wing configurations of each airplane made it much more difficult for each pilot to see the other plane. As they both entered their landing patterns at the same time, one above the other, neither was aware of the other's existence. The standard approach for a landing was to enter the final leg of a rectangular pattern at a forty-five-degree angle on the downwind leg.

The airport was uncontrolled, and there was no radio transmission from the tower. Spectators, including family members of the pilots, were aware of what was happening, but there was no way for them to communicate with either pilot. Some of the people watching the tragedy develop attempted to wave the airplanes away from each other, but the pilots merely waved in return, until it was too late. The Bonanza barely touched the wing of the high-winged Cessna below it, causing it to crash. When I arrived at the airport for my lesson, both the instructor and my substitute were dead.

Sometimes we are given a "wake-up call" that reminds us that life truly is tenuous. This incident instilled in me a sense of gratitude and an obligation to try to make the best use possible of the extra years I had been given. It also dampened my enthusiasm for flying private airplanes.

NICE DOG

Louise Newman

Cousin Louise had called from Bloomington, Indiana, to tell us about a professor at the University of Indiana's School of Music who had been scheduled to deliver a master's class in Europe. A couple of days prior to beginning her journey, her dog suffered an injury. She had purchased the tickets and had made extensive plans for the trip, and she was terribly upset over the prospect of missing the opportunity to travel.

Many friends called with offers to care for her pet during her absence, but she felt compelled to refuse them. She was unwilling to compromise her love for her dog and would not leave it in its precarious condition.

A few days later, she canceled her trip to Paris on Trans World Airlines Flight 800. It departed from Kennedy Airport on July 19, 1996, and crashed twenty miles south of Morishes Bay, New York. Of the 229 passengers, there were no survivors.

How often are we repaid for selfless acts?

MT. HERMON

George W. King

George W. King is a good friend and an outstanding lay leader of a group of Memphis Baptists who are very supportive of Israel. He is a retired businessman who for years has devoted himself to his church, as well as to a study of biblical archeology and history. We met at the University of Memphis while attending a lecture presented by Dr. Aryeh Kasher of Tel-Aviv University. (See "The Telephone Call," p.36.) His church, Kirby Woods Baptist, continues to provide ambulances and other humanitarian aid to Israel. Recently he helped organize a meeting of Christian ministers at the church and asked me to introduce an Israeli dignitary to the assembly. After I related the previous story to him (See "Nice Dog," p.5.), George proceeded to tell of his own experience while on a trip to the Holy Land in December 1988.

When traveling to the Middle East, he enjoys visiting historical sites. If possible, he spends at least one night at each. On one trip, while resting under the stars at Massada, the site of the former encampment of the Roman Tenth Legion (two thousand years earlier), George made the decision to postpone his flight home, which was scheduled for the following day. He called the airline to make the change and proceeded to drive to the summit of Mt. Hermon on the Golan Heights. He wished to witness sunrise from the highest mountain in the country. (Mt. Hermon is located in the northeast corner of Israel and is over 9,200 feet above sea level; it is mentioned numerous times in the Bible, including Psalms 89 and 133.)

"It was a cold night up there," he related, "so I remained in my rental car. To keep warm I would periodically turn on the motor and heater, and every time I started the engine, the radio played. In the early hours of the morning, I heard an interruption of the radio program with news that an airplane had crashed, resulting in great loss of life." George suddenly felt a sinking feeling in his stomach when he realized it was the airplane on which he had been scheduled to return to the United States.

He had cancelled his reservation for Pan American Flight 103, which was destroyed by Libyan terrorists over Lockerbie, Scotland, on December 21, 1988. In that tragedy, 259 passengers lost their lives, in addition to 11 people on the ground.

What induced George to travel so far to witness a sunrise? Perhaps he was meant to live so that he would be able to continue his good works.

BREAD CAST UPON THE WATER

Irma Sheon

For many years my cousins Bob (Dr. Robert) and Irma Sheon from Toledo, Ohio, and five or six other couples often spent a few days each summer playing tennis and visiting the Stratford Festival in Stratford, Canada.

A few years ago, one of the couples discovered their son Eric was in kidney failure. After some months of dialysis treatment, his mother Anita was tested and found to be a suitable kidney donor for her son. Sadly, before the surgery could be scheduled, she became ill and was diagnosed with ovarian cancer. She died a few weeks after the diagnosis, but before Anita's death, Irma began the steps necessary to become a living kidney donor. Weeks after the funeral, Irma learned that her blood type matched that of Eric, whom she had never met. From that moment she considered the situation *beshert*, and further testing led to the donation of her kidney on her sixty-sixth birthday.

But that is not the end of the story, for in testing Irma as a prospective donor, the doctors advised that there was an aneurysm of the artery leading to her spleen. Further tests suggested the need for surgical removal of the aneurysm, an operation that probably saved her from a sudden tragedy.

As you might have surmised, the Sheons are an outstanding couple. They have devoted many years to helping others in so many ways, and their wonderful children have followed in their footsteps. The fortunate discovery of Irma's medical condition following her organ donation is a poignant example of synchronicity at work.

THE BLESSING

Charles Steinberg

We were at a bowling alley in November 1999, helping to celebrate the sixtieth birthday of our friend Ronald Harkavy, when I spied my old friend Charles Steinberg. (See "R and R," p.24.) He didn't look very well. He was desperate to obtain a liver replacement and was reconciled to the fact that if one didn't become available soon, he would not have much time. I knew of his precarious condition and the fact that a person his age would have little chance of obtaining a liver replacement.

As I looked about the room that night, I spotted Rabbi Efraim Greenblatt. Since he was planning a trip to Israel soon, I asked if he might say a special prayer for Charles at the Western Wall in Jerusalem, the holiest site in the Jewish world. (The good rabbi is considered a very holy individual, not only by the entire Memphis community, both Jewish and secular, but also by people around the world who have read his scholarly books *Revivos Efraim* and have come to know and love him.)

He asked Charles his mother's name in Hebrew, the one used to petition G-d on behalf of a desperately ill person. A few days later in Israel, he wrote the prayer on a piece of paper and placed it in a crevice in the Holy Wall in Jerusalem. When he returned from his trip, the rabbi called to see how his friend was feeling. Charles asked him to recall when the request was inserted in the "Wall." After some discussion, they determined that within an hour of that act, Charles was called to go immediately to the hospital for his new liver.

At age sixty-five, Charles was the oldest recipient of a liver transplant in our community. Since that time he has spent countless hours reassuring prospective recipients as well as organ donors. He advises nurses and physicians from the perspective of transplant patients. He serves weekly as a volunteer for the local Ronald McDonald House and remains a Diamond Life Master bridge player.

SHARING

Rabbi Efraim Greenblatt

In Tel Aviv there lived a very poor family. During a desperate time, the husband went from house to house seeking food for his starving family. After numerous rejections, he arrived at a residence where he pleaded for something to eat on behalf of his children and his wife. The man of the house explained, "All week long my family and I live only on bread and water, and it is only on the Sabbath that we each enjoy one piece of chicken. I really wish I could help you, but we have just enough for ourselves." As the supplicant continued to plead for help, the man was deeply touched. Determining that the begging man's family was in even worse financial condition than his, he agreed to share one of the two chickens he had saved for Friday night's dinner. When he opened the door of the freezer to obtain the chicken, he found his two-year-old son inside, crying. As the child was playing, the door had closed and he had become trapped. His life was spared thanks to his father's act of *tzedakah* (righteousness).

There is a verse in Deuteronomy that commands us to be generous in sharing our blessings. It tells us to give again and again, and because we give, G-d will bless us in all that we do.
A book could be written of the many known good deeds that Rabbi Greenblatt has performed. He is a living sanctification of G-d's name.
Rabbi Greenblatt has assured me of the authenticity of this fascinating story.

THE WARNING

Oscar Goldberg

Fifty years ago, Paul Goldberg, the father of my friend and fraternity brother Oscar Goldberg, received a telephone call from his wife Bessie. She had traveled to West Virginia to visit cousins, and later that evening for some reason she could not understand, she felt uneasy about her husband. He was sleeping in their second-floor apartment in St. Louis, Missouri. Bessie felt a compulsion to call her family, although it was a time when people of modest means rarely placed long distance calls. She asked her husband repeatedly if everything was all right, and he continued to respond affirmatively. "Of course everything is all right. Why do you keep asking?" he queried. A few minutes after their conversation ended, smoke began pouring into his apartment; a fire had started in the basement.

Why had she chosen that moment to call? What was it that created her anxiety?

THE WORLD TRADE CENTER

Jerome Makowsky

Many fascinating stories have circulated since September 11, 2001, and many more will continue to be newsworthy. There is one told of the bus carrying a large group of men who worked at the World Trade Center. It had developed engine trouble that day, delaying its arrival at a critical moment. There is the tale of a former Memphis resident who answered a call that morning to participate in a *minyan* (a quorum of ten or more Jewish males over the age of thirteen, required for the recitation of certain prayers). He subsequently arrived at his WTC office a half-hour after the disaster. One of the most intriguing incidents told to us was this one, which was brought from New York by my friend Jerome Makowsky.

It seems that during late August of 2001, an observant Jewish man brought his *t'fillin* to a *sofer* (scribe) in Elizabeth, New Jersey, to be examined. (*T'fillin* are small leather boxes attached with leather straps and donned each morning, except Saturdays, by males over the age of thirteen prior to praying. One is placed upon the forehead and the other on the upper arm. They contain segments of Hebrew scripture, and users are directed in accordance with a verse in Deuteronomy that they "be bound for a sign upon thy hand and shall be for frontlets between thine eyes." Periodically they are examined by competent individuals to determine if the drying ink has created gaps in the letters, thereby rendering the *t'fillin* ritually unfit.) On Sunday, September 10, the man arranged to pick them up early the next morning in New Jersey. He felt he would have time to get them prior to going to his job at the World Trade Center. Due to heavy traffic problems, he was delayed while driving into Manhattan, and his life was spared. Several weeks later, he telephoned the sofer to determine the condition of his *t'fillin* and was advised that they seemed to be in good shape. "In fact," he was told, "the only place that needed attention was *L'ma'an Yirbu Y'meichem*" (Deut.21.) In essence, it says that if one does these things that have been commanded, "[Your] days and those of your children shall be multiplied."

THE CANDLE

Harry Samuels

For many years, every Friday prior to sunset, my wife lit some candles that formally inaugurated the Sabbath. When we were first married, she lit one candle for each of us and as our sons were born, she added candles, designating only in her mind that individual represented by each candle.

From the Friday our son David was diagnosed with cancer and every week for eighteen months thereafter, whenever she lit them, the one she had designated for David either went out or burned out long before all the others. We tried moving the menorah (candlestick holder) to different parts of the room and even froze the candles at one time, but to no avail.

Even now, sixteen years later, when candles are lit, his is almost always the first to go out. I mentioned this phenomenon to someone else who had lost a child. He said the same thing happened to him and his wife for the thirty days following their child's death.

Here we have another suspension of what we perceive to be the natural order.

THE MORNING SERVICE

Harry Samuels

For five days each week—Monday through Friday—they met near their places of work early in the morning to pray. One day they stood in the alcove of a structure surrounded by tall, gray concrete and steel buildings, searching for another Jewish man. The nine men worked in the same place, and it was a convenient way to conform to their religious practice of morning prayers before beginning work. But today they needed a tenth man for a religious quorum in order to recite certain prayers.

They had almost given up the idea of finding another person when a stranger approached. "I will be glad to join you," he said, "but I have a request. It is my father's *yahrzeit*, the anniversary of his death, and in his memory I would like to lead the service." They reluctantly agreed; however, the stranger was so slow in reading the Hebrew that several of the "regulars" became quite agitated. They were afraid they would be late for work unless the old man started moving at a faster speed. Suddenly they heard a tremendous crash nearby.

It was September 11, 2001, and their workplace, the World Trade Center, had just been attacked. Had the stranger been able to read faster, they would have been inside the building.

How often does a good deed benefit the initiator as well as the one for whom it is intended—perhaps more often than we realize.

I first heard this story delivered in a public forum by Cantor Aryeh Samberg. He said he couldn't vouch for its origin since he had heard it from someone else. Subsequently, unrelated individuals have repeated it with assurances of its validity.

THE BAND LEADER

Dr. Stanley Frager

My nephew Stanley Frager organized a dance band while he was a youngster in high school in University City, Missouri. The band, which was made up of close-knit friends, became extremely popular. It ultimately played a significant role in saving his life. In 1975, Stanley convinced his father to accompany him overseas for a vacation. During that trip, his dad saw evidence of Stanley's rectal bleeding. "What on earth is this, Stan?" his dad asked.

"I don't believe it is anything serious," he replied, "but if it will make you happy, I'll have someone look at it when we return to the United States."

When he returned to Louisville, Stanley failed to call a doctor. Still attributing the problem to hemorrhoids, he saw no urgency in making an appointment for an examination. His father, however, badgered him, calling him daily from St. Louis until Stanley saw a physician. The doctor immediately diagnosed his problem as advanced colon cancer that required immediate surgery. He also conveyed the grim news that the mortality rate for the illness was extremely high.

One of the first persons Stanley called to tell about the prognosis was his old friend Alan Spivak. Alan, along with his brother Sam, had played in Stan's band, and the three had remained lifelong friends. Alan told Stan that his brother, an oncologist practicing in San Francisco at Sinai Hospital, was currently researching a new method of radiating cancer sites prior to surgery. The doctors had had some success with a couple of patients. Stanley's doctor in Louisville concluded that there was little risk in trying the radiation prior to surgery, a common practice now, but still experimental twenty-eight years ago. The treatment and surgery were completed in 1975, and Stanley is still making music and enjoying life, thanks in great part to a drummer and baritone saxophone player in his old band.

Dr. Stanley R. Frager is a professor of psychology at the University of Louisville. He is the author of the book The Champion within You: How to Overcome Problems, Obstacles, and Adversity in Your Life, *and is a highly regarded motivational speaker. Dr. Frager has had an interesting life, during which he hosted a radio talk* show in Louisville, Kentucky, for many years that was beamed to over thirty states. Additionally, he has worked with Olympic athletes, earning accolades from major sports publications, and he has served as a volunteer assistant baseball coach and as a member of the prep band at the University of Louisville (as its only faculty member). He has accomplished all of these feats while continuing to lead the largest Boy Scout troop in Kentucky and maintaining an active practice as a licensed psychologist. He often heads cancer drives for the city of Louisville and the state of Kentucky. At the time of the Watts riots in California, he served as a probation officer for the state while studying for his doctoral degree. During that period, he was credited with helping to quell a serious uprising at a local penal institution, subjecting himself to considerable personal risk.

THE MATCHBOOK

Dr. Pierre Secher

Dr. Pierre Secher was born and reared in Vienna, Austria. His father Emil had come to the city in 1886, and the family had lived there comfortably until the rise of Adolph Hitler. During the early 1930s, a cousin by the name of Herman Handel traveled to Vienna on a vacation from America. Emil was quite hospitable to his visitor, showing him beautiful pre-war Vienna in all its splendor. Herman was appreciative of the hospitality shown to him, and prior to returning home, he tossed Emil a matchbook. It displayed the name of his cafeteria in Newark, New Jersey. He added, "When you come to the United States, please look us up so we can reciprocate your kindness." Emil thanked him, throwing the matches into a box.

In July of 1938, it became apparent that remaining in Austria was not a good option for Jewish families. The Sechers registered for visas to come to America. At that time they were told that there would be a waiting period of eighteen months.

"On September 1, 1939, the Nazis marched into Poland to begin World War II. I was listening to Hitler on the radio that day," said Pierre. "As the declaration of war was being announced, the postman rang our doorbell. He had brought the required papers for the precious visas; however, there was still a requirement to be met prior to their final issuance. The United States was in the midst of the Great Depression. Its government insisted on guarantees from local American citizens that newcomers would not become financial burdens on the country. Without these guarantees, the final papers could not be obtained." As immigration was about to be stopped completely, the Sechers searched frantically for the address of their American relatives. At last they found the box into which it had been thrown years earlier. When the American cousins were reached, they immediately arranged for the required vouchers, and the lives of the Sechers were saved—in part by a matchbook, which allowed them to contact the visitors to whom they had once extended kindness.

Dr. Pierre Secher, a former professor of political science, has recently completed his book Left Behind in Nazi Vienna: Letters of a Jewish Family Caught in the Holocaust 1939–1941.

PART II
ARMED SERVICES

FRATERNITY BROTHER

Harry Samuels

Prior to my reassignment in 1953, in the United States Army at Aberdeen Proving Grounds, I was placed into a holding detachment with two thousand others. I was an enlisted man and was feeling pretty lonely and blue. Armed with a weekend pass, I rushed to get away from the post and decided to head for College Park, Maryland, home of the University of Maryland. Recalling that there was a chapter of my college fraternity, Sigma Alpha Mu, at that school, I thought it might be an opportunity to meet some friendly guys and, even better, some girls. After negotiating the heavy traffic, I finally located the fraternity house but found no one at home. A neighbor said they had all gone to a football game. Since the front door was unlocked, I entered, and for the first time in days, I began to feel relaxed. I had graduated from Washington University in St. Louis, Missouri, a year earlier, and as a member of that fraternity, I felt no compunction about entering the house. After writing some despondent letters, I proceeded to "sack out" upstairs in someone's bunk. A short time later, the doorbell rang, and I rushed downstairs to see a man walking away from the front door. After calling to him, he turned around, and for a moment we both were temporarily transfixed.

It was Edward Feldman, one of my college fraternity brothers. We hadn't been in touch since entering the service. For the previous year, he had served in the Presidential Honor Guard at Ft. Meyer, Virginia, and had never before been to the University of Maryland. We had both come at the same time—and reconnected.

Edward Feldman and I have remained close friends for fifty-six years. Flora and I often speak with him and his lovely wife Barbara, and we enjoy traveling with them.

R and R

Charles Steinberg

Charles Steinberg once mentioned an incident during the Korean War in 1952 while he was serving in the United States Army. He was stationed near the front and had gone to Kimpa Air Force Base to "catch a ride" on an airplane that transported front-line personnel to Tokyo for well-earned rest and recreation. He vividly recalled, "The planes left every four hours and held almost three hundred people. I was really irritated. I had just missed catching an earlier flight but was told I would be number twenty-six for the next one. We finally boarded the plane and landed in the big city. When we arrived in Tokyo, we learned that the earlier flight, the one I had just missed, had crashed, killing all those aboard. It was the biggest airplane disaster of that year."

Perhaps we should not be so disappointed when our wishes are not granted.

THE DISAPPOINTMENT

Bert Bornblum

At the beginning of World War II, Bert Bornblum joined the United States Army Air Corps. He was born and reared in Warsaw, Poland, and had only recently come to the United States. He tried very diligently to speak English correctly, but it was difficult since he had the handicap of a strong Yiddish accent.

An intelligence test was given to all new recruits in order to determine the job for which they would be best suited. He scored well on all the tests that were administered, and the Army placed him in the signal corps. Bert excelled in mastering all of the non-verbal skills required, but when he was given verbal communication tasks, the men to whom he attempted to speak couldn't understand him. They complained of his inability to communicate properly. Some thought he was a German soldier who had infiltrated their outfit.

He was disappointed when he was transferred from his unit, but he had no choice in the matter. Bert was reassigned to another unit in which it was felt his talents might be better used and in which his accent would not prove to be such a barrier. As time progressed, he was eventually sent to the European Theater of Operations while everyone in his former unit was sent to the Pacific Theater.

After the war, he met a friend who had served in the South Pacific and had been in touch with Bert's former outfit. It was then that he learned that not a single member of his former group had survived the war.

Perhaps he was saved by his Jewish accent, not such a handicap after all!

Bert and his brother David settled in Memphis, Tennessee. There, through years of diligent effort, they achieved financial success in the retail business. Both have expressed gratitude for their good fortune and have attempted to repay society in various ways. They have established significant endowments in several non-profit foundations of the city, including one at the University of Memphis. Both men continue to serve as volunteers on numerous boards.

BORROWED SHOES

Murray Habbaz

Sam Beyda was riding on a commuter train from Washington, D.C., to New York City during World War II. The train was very crowded. The passengers were not eager to share their spaces with strangers, but since the seat next to him was empty, Sam invited a young sailor to join him. He asked the sailor if he were going east to embark for the European Theater of Operations. "No," came the reply, "I have been stationed in the Far Pacific on a ship, and I am going home to New York to begin a thirty-day leave."

"That seems like a great vacation, but why so long? Is that normal?"

"Actually," the sailor said, "thirty days is given to anyone on a ship that is sunk, and that is what happened to ours." He proceeded to apprise Sam of the details following the sinking of his ship. "As we were going down, I took off my clothing, grabbed an inflatable lifejacket, and jumped into the choppy water. Fortunately, we were very close to an island that had just been captured from Japanese defenders by a detachment of United States Marines. In fact, I owe my life to one of them who happened to be a wonderful swimmer. When I found myself in the water, I realized my lifejacket had failed to inflate and that I was beginning to sink. Surely I would have drowned had it not been for the heroic effort of a marine who swam out to save me. He was a great guy, and since we were the same size, he even gave me some clothing to replace the clothes I had left in the ocean. I can even tell you who he was since these shoes I am wearing still have his name and serial number on them," he said, presenting a shoe for examination.

"It can't be," Sam gasped. "I don't believe it. They are my son's shoes!"

Extending oneself often leads to a meaningful connection.

THE SNAKE CHARMER

Dr. Edward Berg

In 1968, while Dr. Edward Berg was stationed in Viet Nam, he and another physician on leave traveled to Delhi, India. One day, while standing in front of the Red Fort (a well-known landmark in Delhi), Ed was approached by a snake charmer who wished to tell his fortune. Edward told the man that he was not interested in his predictions or assessments and that he certainly didn't intend to pay for any unsolicited services. The snake charmer said he thought Ed might change his mind if he gave him a chance to display his talents. He proceeded to state, correctly, that Ed's mother's name was Ruth. He further predicted that Ed was going to marry a girl whose first name contained five letters and began with the letter "M."

Three years later in California, Ed bumped into his old traveling companion who asked if the prediction made in Delhi had come true. It was then that Ed introduced him to his wife Maris. (See "Banking in L.A.," p.47.)

Dr. Edward Berg is an assistant clinical professor at the Washington University School of Medicine in St. Louis, and he also maintains a private practice in the city. He and his family have traveled to Third World countries as volunteers. They continue to help improve the standard of living of many of those who are less fortunate. He is my nephew.

THE DINNER INVITATION

E. J. Goldsmith, Jr.

A couple of years ago, I was asked to deliver a talk on the subject of synchronicity as it relates to some of these stories. Before speaking to approximately fifty adults, I mentioned the fact that I planned to include some of the anecdotes in a book if I were able to obtain a sufficient number of them for publication. I also solicited additional stories from the audience. After indicating that the stories they were going to hear would probably reflect some of their own experiences, I asked them to share any anecdotes they thought to be interesting. I suggested that if they were willing to contribute stories, it might be a way for them to attain a bit of immortality since I intended to give proper attribution to each person whose story we published. On the other hand, I pointed out, if they wished to achieve immortality on their own, I would use their stories without mentioning their names. At the end of the program, I again requested the participation of the audience, but could find none. As I was leaving, an old friend Elias Goldsmith, now of blessed memory, called me aside and offered a story he thought might qualify for my book.

He told of a time during World War II in the early 1940s when he was stationed at Fort Bragg, North Carolina. "It was Mother's Day," he said, "and my mother came for a visit that Sunday. We were on our way to dinner when Mom noticed a sergeant standing alone next to a telephone pole about twenty feet from us. 'Would you like to join us for dinner?' she inquired. 'I surely would,' he replied, 'it's pretty lonely here on weekends.'" After eating, the sergeant asked if Elias liked his job. "No sergeant," he answered, "they are teaching me how to cut barbed-wire, and I am definitely not interested in learning that skill. But why do you ask?"

"I am personnel sergeant for this division, and perhaps I could get you transferred into a different unit," he answered. A couple of weeks later, Elias was transferred to another group. He ultimately entered officers' training and was a captain at the war's end. Later he learned that his former unit had landed on

Omaha Beach in Normandy at the time of the invasion of France and that not a single member of that unit had survived.

Mr. Goldsmith was of diminutive size but enormous character. He was involved in many organizations for the benefit of the city of Memphis and its inhabitants and was greatly loved by those who knew him. Our community owes that sergeant a debt of thanks.

PART III
IN ISRAEL

THE ABORTION

Harry Samuels

Rabbi Aryeh Levin (1885–1969) was a pious and modest man who lived in one of the poorest sections of Jerusalem until his death. He was affectionately known as Reb Aryeh. He spent every Sabbath ministering to prisoners instead of attending his own synagogue services. He was often referred to as the "Rabbi of the Prisoners." (See *A Tzaddik in Our Times* by Simcha Raz.) Two years ago his grandson Rabbi Benjamin Levene shared this remarkable story with us.

Reb Aryeh was considered such a learned and holy man that when the chief rabbi of Israel was unavailable, questions of *Halacha* (Jewish law) were referred to him. One day the son of some old friends called upon him, requesting a favor. The man was a member of the Knesset, the national legislature, and he said he was there to plead for a couple desiring an abortion. "They are poor people with a house full of children and do not see how they will be able to manage with an addition to their large family. Won't you please grant them their request?" he implored. Reb Aryeh pointed out repeatedly that the Jewish faith clearly supports the saving of life, not its destruction. An abortion would be allowed only under very limited circumstances. (In order to save a life, every law in the sacred Torah is *required* to be broken except for the prohibitions against murder, incest and idolatry.) The visitor remained insistent until finally Reb Aryeh said he wished to tell him a story of a similar situation.

"Years ago," he began, "another couple came to me with the same request and under comparable circumstances. They did not know where their next meal was coming from. I told them that my heart went out to them, but that as much as I wished to be of help, in that instance I could do nothing. Do you believe I answered them appropriately?" he queried. "I don't understand," the man responded, "you know why I am here. Why do you ask this question?" "Because," the good rabbi said, "they were your parents."

One of the most interesting and nicest individuals we have met is Rabbi Benjamin (Benji) Levene, the grandson of Rabbi Aryeh Levin. Benji is an executive with

Gesher, *a wonderful organization domiciled in Jerusalem and dedicated to bridging differences among various Jewish religious streams. The word* gesher *in Hebrew means* bridge. *Benji lives in Jerusalem and treats visitors to tours of his famous grandfather's world. In December 2002, he showed my wife and me where his grandfather had lived and prayed, and he shared the memorable previous story. Benji also mentioned that when his aunt, Rabbi Aryeh's daughter, was desperately ill, the prisoners to whom he ministered wanted to be of help. They petitioned G-d, requesting that portions of their lives each be shortened by an amount that would then be added to hers. Whether one agrees with this gesture or not, the fact remains that she lived well into her nineties. According to her nephew, she was not too pleased with those prisoners during her later difficult years.*

To help sensitize those Jews with opposing ideological differences, Benji has developed a fascinating one-man show, The Four Faces of Israel. *The stereotypes he poignantly portrays demonstrate fundamental differences, leaving each with a better understanding of the other.*
Following his presentation in 1998 in Memphis, my wife and I hosted a brunch at our home to allow supporters of Gesher *to meet him. Benji had just presented me with a biography of his legendary grandfather when I introduced him to Rabbi Levi Klein, the spiritual leader of the local Chabad Lubavitch congregation. "Are you the grandson of the late Rabbi Menachem Klein of Jerusalem?" asked Benji. (See "Caracas," p.85.) "Yes," replied Rabbi Klein. "He was a close friend of Reb Aryeh and is mentioned there," he said, pointing to my newly acquired book.*

Rabbi Menachem Klein and Reb Aryeh would have been delighted to know their grandsons had finally met.
Gesher *is located at 10 King David Street Jerusalem, 94101, Israel. E-mail: gesher @gesher.co.il*

THE BUS LINE

Malky Shine

The Jewish family lived in Poland prior to World War II, and several siblings managed to escape the Holocaust. Esther and Paul spent the war in a Russian labor camp and then in Germany before finally settling in St. Paul, Minnesota. Each of Esther's two sisters came to Israel, unaware that the other had survived the war. Leah settled in Hertzalia while her sister Henia moved to Mitzeret Elite near Tiberius. Almost twenty years passed before they spotted each other while both were in line at a bus station in Haifa.

THE TELEPHONE CALL

Dr. Aryeh and Tamar Kasher

A telephone operator from Tel-Aviv was asked to place a telephone call to someone in the Negev Desert near Be'er-Sheva. She completed the call and reached another telephone operator, with whom she made a connection (no pun intended). The two enjoyed speaking with each other, and after that chance conversation, whenever they found some free time, they would call each other to chat.

One day the lady from Tel-Aviv suggested, "When you come shopping next Thursday, please come to our home for lunch. I am anxious to meet you and for you to meet my husband, parents, and children." After lunch the lady from Be'er-Sheva asked where her host's parents had previously lived. "These are not my biological parents. My parents were killed in the Holocaust, and these people adopted me when I was a small child. As a matter of fact," she offered, while removing and opening a small locket from her neck, "this is the only vestige of my past that I have." Pointing to one side of the locket, she continued, "I was told this was a picture of me that was found in my locket when I first arrived." Pointing to the photograph on the other side of the locket, she declared it to be a picture of her sister whom she had never met. Immediately the other lady removed a similar locket displaying the same pictures.

Dr. Kasher is a professor of history at Tel-Aviv University and a recognized authority of the Second Temple Period. His interest in ancient history stems from an experience he had while serving in the Israeli Armored Corps. At the end of their training, members of that group traditionally climbed to the summit of Massada where they spent the night and were formally inducted into the corps. The next morning, he was the last to leave the mountain top and was given the task of seeing that nothing remained from their visit. As he was leaving, he noticed a bit of tarnished metal on the ground and brought it home as a souvenir. After polishing it, he realized it was a coin from two thousand years earlier, left perhaps by one of the last defenders of the site who had opted to commit suicide rather than submit to the subjugation of the Roman Tenth

Legion. He contacted the Department of Antiquities; its officials allowed him to keep the coin. As he learned more about its history, he developed an intense interest in what became his life's work.

JERUSALEM

Harry Samuels

It no longer seems unusual to find mutual friends among strangers we meet while traveling in the United States and overseas. My wife and I are only surprised when it *doesn't* happen.

In 1993 we were sightseeing in Jerusalem with our good friends, Marty and Laverne (Tootie) Hecht from Cape Girardeau, Missouri, and Irv and Cecelia (Teedy) Applebaum, from La Jolla, California. They told us about a television program produced by *National Geographic.* The topic was a home located near the remaining remnant of the Second Holy Temple, a retaining wall known as the *Kotel,* or Western Wall, built approximately 2,400 years earlier. The owners of the home, Mr. and Mrs. Theo Siebenberg, were convinced that by virtue of its location, it rested on interesting and potentially productive archeological artifacts. They proceeded to excavate the property.

As they had predicted, many fascinating items, dating back several millennia were discovered below their property. They included rings made two thousand years earlier that unlocked jewelry and cosmetic cases. The owners had moved into the upper floor of their home while making the lower portion into a non-profit museum.

We didn't know their names or the location of the house and spent time trying to locate a place with which no one seemed familiar. At last we found the Siebenberg Home and met the friendly owners. We invited the couple to dine with us that evening at the King David Hotel, and during the course of our conversation, we learned that she had been born and reared in Jerusalem while Theo was from Antwerp, Belgium. I noted that I only knew one person who was from Belgium, someone with whom I had served in the United States Army during the Korean War. When I mentioned his name, Theo told us that he was a close personal friend and that he had spoken with him in America two days earlier.

TIBERIAS

Harry Samuels

Our family had arrived in Tiberias, Israel, late in the afternoon during July 1981. It was our first visit, and we wanted to see as much of that ancient city as possible as we were only there for one day. As soon as we checked into our hotel, we proceeded to explore the area. Passing an ice cream shop, I noticed a young man wearing a University of Tennessee shirt. I assumed he was an Israeli, but when I asked in Hebrew if he attended UT, he replied in English that he was Lee Baum from Memphis, Tennessee, and that he knew us. We were friends of his parents, Phillip and Joan Baum. Flora had played tennis with his mother a few days earlier. Lee and the fellow next to him had just graduated from college and were taking in the sights prior to getting serious with their lives. I asked his friend where he lived and he said, "Chattanooga, Tennessee." I said that I knew only one person who was from there, a wonderful elderly friend, Harry Trotz. "He is my grandfather," he replied.

Harry Trotz was quite a man. His father was conscripted into the Russian army at the time Harry's mother died giving birth to her sixth child. At the tender age of twelve, Harry, as the oldest child, became the head of his family. He refused to allow his siblings to become separated. He nurtured and protected all of them until his father returned.

FAMILY

Dr. Aryeh and Tamar Kasher

During lunch in Jerusalem last year, Professor and Mrs. Kasher (See "The Telephone Call," p.36.) reminded us of an incident that had occurred years earlier at the home of their cousins in Tel-Aviv. Following World War II, their cousins adopted an eleven-year-old boy. Much later, when the child had grown into manhood, his adopted family held a party to which the Kashers were invited. When an elderly lady arrived, the adoptee asked Dr. Kasher if he knew her. "She is a cousin," Kasher offered, "but why do you ask?"

"She seems so familiar," he replied. Later, the young man approached the lady and introduced himself. He asked if she had ever been to Warsaw, Poland, prior to the war.

"Yes," she replied, "I went to visit some of my family who lived there, but unfortunately none of them survived the war."

It was then that he realized where he had seen the lady. At that moment the inquisitive young man understood that he had been adopted by members of his own family.

ENTEBBE

Harry Samuels

On June 27, 1976, Arab and German terrorists hijacked an Air France commercial airplane en route to Entebbe, Uganda. On the plane were over one hundred Israelis, in addition to Jewish men and women from other countries. They were immediately segregated and placed under guard at the airport terminal. The terrorists announced they intended to begin executing hostages on July 3, 1976, unless Israel released fifty terrorist prisoners. Israel subsequently mounted a daring commando raid under the command of Lieutenant Colonel Jonathan "Yoni" Netanyahu that succeeded in flying 2,000 miles and rescuing all of the prisoners except one. The only soldier lost was Colonel Netanyahu.

Years later, my wife and I had lunch in Memphis with a retired Israeli air force general who had flown one of the four planes on that mission. He shared this fascinating story with us—one that to my knowledge has not been published.

He told us that initial plans called for men to parachute near the Entebbe airfield in order to secure it for the rescue airplanes. Since the guards at the terminal building held grenades and machine guns, it was important to overwhelm them before they could kill the hostages. A few days prior to the mission, an Israeli parachutist came to see his commanding officer. The soldier adamantly refused to go on the mission as it was planned. When asked the reason, he said he had been reading about Uganda and learned there were alligators in the body of water near the airfield where they were to descend. He was not interested in attacking at night under those conditions. That evening, the officers took a break from their planning efforts to watch international news on television. They saw President Idi Amin of Uganda arriving at the terminal in a large black Mercedes limousine with sirens blaring. His car was flanked and led by motorcycle outriders. The Israelis immediately decided to locate a couple of similar automobiles, load them into their Hercules airplanes, along with some motorcycles and soldiers, and attempt to replicate the scene they had just witnessed on television. They felt that by basing their efforts on stealth and surprise, the guards might think Amin was returning to the airport. The problem that then arose was in locating some limousines. They called Avis and Budget; both offered many Subarus and Toyotas but no Mercedes. Someone noticed an advertisement in the classified section of the newspaper. An Arab from East Jerusalem offered two white Mercedes limousines for lease. The men spray-painted them black, and the rest is history.

How many lives were saved as a result of that television program?

LOST

Marlin Graber

The late Lillian Feldman moved from Helena, Arkansas, to Memphis, Tennessee, and joined the faculty of the Margolin Hebrew Academy. It was there that Marlin and Evelyn Graber met her, and they became good friends. One summer Marlin and Evelyn decided to visit Israel. They stayed at the Sheraton Hotel in Jerusalem and were pleased to learn that Lillian, too, was spending the summer in that city.

The Grabers wished to see Eilat which is located in the southernmost part of Israel on the Gulf of Aqaba. They planned to travel in a small commuter airplane but learned that its tiny airport was located in an area north of Jerusalem. They were unfamiliar with the route, and they told Lillian that they feared they would have trouble finding the place. She offered to take them in her car, but in doing so, became hopelessly lost. They noticed two Arab men dressed in traditional regalia walking along the road. Stopping the car and rolling down the window, she asked, "Can you direct us to the airport?"

One of the strangers replied, "Lillian, aren't you a long way from home?"

It was a man who had lived in Helena, Arkansas, and he had known Lillian and her family.

The world is quite small.

PART IV
TRAVELS

BANKING IN LOS ANGELES

Maris Frager Berg

After graduating from Washington University in St. Louis, Missouri, my niece Maris Frager was hired by a hospital in Los Angeles, California, as an occupational therapist. She drove to the West Coast, and while on the freeway, she remembered she had very little cash. Noticing a bank sign in the distance, she exited the highway and entered the building. She went into the bank to cash a fifty-dollar check drawn on her St. Louis bank account. As the lines became shorter, she moved from one to the other until she finally stood before a teller.

"Hello, my name is Maris Frager, and I would like to cash a check for fifty dollars," she said. "I have just arrived in Los Angeles and have not yet established a banking relationship, but I have been hired by a local hospital as an occupational therapist and can show you a letter confirming that fact." She presented her driver's license and the letter of acceptance. The teller looked at her license and confirmed that she was from St. Louis.

The next question came as a shock: "Do you know Rose or Al Frager from St. Louis?"

"Of course," Maris replied, "they are my parents."

The bank employee, Mrs. Stern, had known her mother for many years in Cape Girardeau, Missouri. She not only cashed the check, but she invited Maris for dinner.

What were the chances of this interchange occurring in what was then the second largest city of the United States?

TURKEY

Harold Newburger

Dena Newburger had just completed a year of study at Hebrew University in Jerusalem. She planned to travel to Turkey with a friend who changed her mind at the last minute. Instead, Dena's father Hal Newburger decided to accompany her on the trip.

While sitting on a bench of a ferry in Turkey, Hal asked a stranger sitting on the same bench if he would watch their personal items while he proceeded to take a picture of his daughter from a different spot. The man agreed. Upon their return, the stranger said, "You certainly must be a very trusting soul since I could have walked away with all your things."

"Of course," replied Hal, "we are from Memphis, Tennessee, which is in the United States, and we trust people there. My name is Hal Newburger, and this is my daughter Dena."

"I know," the young man responded. "I once spent a week as a guest in your home."

In 1983, the Memphis Jewish Community Center hosted the first North American Junior Macabbi Games; Dena's mother Ronna was president at that time. Hospitality was provided by Memphians for hundreds of young teenagers from around the world, including this young man from Israel.

ALBANY

Harry Samuels

Our son Marty had been accepted to Rensselaer Polytechnic Institute, and he and I traveled to Troy, New York, to see the facility. While staying in nearby Albany, we called the home of Dr. and Mrs. Bob Hoffman. Dr. Hoffman was an arthritic specialist. We had recently met his children in Memphis.

The Hoffmans insisted we dine with them that evening. During dinner they asked about our family, and I explained we had all recently traveled to Israel for the bar mitzvah of our youngest son David.

"I don't suppose you had many friends and relatives in attendance there, did you?" they asked.

"As a matter of fact, there were quite a few who joined us, including a young man from Toledo, Ohio, whose father is also an arthritic specialist," I responded.

"What is his name?"

When I told him it was Bob Sheon, he excused himself from the dinner table and returned with a brochure with my cousin's picture on the cover. "I scheduled him to be a guest lecturer at our local medical school," he said. "Had you been here earlier today, you could have spoken with him as I did."

BUYING TRIP

Harry Samuels

In 1968, while managing a discount department store in Memphis, Tennessee, I traveled to New York City to evaluate a new buying office that our firm had purchased. Prior to leaving Memphis, my wife asked where we would be staying, and I told her it would be the Gotham Hotel in Manhattan.

Arriving in New York, I learned the name of the hotel was the Warwick, and I called to give her the correct address. The only association I previously had with the name Gotham was as the name of the metropolis in the *Batman* comic books I had read as a child. Why that name had entered my head was a mystery.

Later that evening some of the store managers invited me to dine with them at a French restaurant located a few blocks from the Museum of Modern Art. Instead of making an evening of it with the others, I returned to my hotel after dinner in order to catch up on some correspondence. Entering the lobby, I felt disoriented and was having trouble finding the elevator, which seemed to be located in the wrong spot. Imagine my shock when I approached the concierge and discovered on his desk a metal plaque imprinted with the name "Gotham Hotel." The hotels were near each other, and I had "accidentally" visited the wrong one.

This episode felt like something from The Twilight Zone. *I still get chills when I think about it.*

THE TROUSERS

Harry Samuels

It was Mother's Day 1999, and we had traveled to St. Louis to help celebrate the seventieth birthday of Sam Fox, a college friend and fraternity brother. It was also the sixty-eighth birthday of my niece Eileen, and prior to leaving Memphis, we had purchased a gift for her on the assumption we would be seeing her at a family function that week. We made an effort, but we couldn't get together.

We spent the next day with some cousins who took us shopping. I purchased a couple of sport coats. Since I needed trousers to go with the coats, we began looking for some in several shopping centers, but to no avail. At 7:00 P.M. that evening, our cousin suggested we check one last store in a different shopping center. She had never visited it, but she had recently seen it advertised. We called to see if the store was open and if it carried the brand of slacks I wanted. When we entered, the store manager, Julie, immediately recognized my wife and me. She is my great niece and the daughter of the niece we had planned to visit.

It was not surprising to find the trousers, but Julie was a little surprised when I asked if she would give her mother the birthday gift we had brought her.

CRUSING 1

Harry Samuels

Toward the end of 1999, we were on a cruise to the Bahamas. It was Saturday, and we had docked in Barbados. We had never been there before. We decided to attend religious services that morning at what was reputed to be the second oldest synagogue in the Western Hemisphere.

Following the short service, the president of the congregation presented a historical review of the synagogue and its adjacent cemetery, which contains gravestones dating back to the fifteenth century.

"Our congregation received some financial assistance for the rehabilitation of our building from the American Jewish Congress," he said.

"Forty-five years ago, during the Korean War, I served in the Army with someone who ultimately assumed an executive position with that organization," I noted. When I mentioned his name, he replied that he had just spoken with him a day earlier. After visiting for a short time, we also determined that we were fraternity brothers.

CRUSING 2

Dr. Albert and Deanna Burson

Dr. Al and Deanna Burson, while on a cruise, stopped at Paradise Island in the Bahamas. They opted to take a water taxi with a large group of others to view the island. Initially they sat behind a couple but subsequently moved to different seats. Again they moved in order to avoid sitting near a busy gangway. Following the last move, Deanna felt compelled to explain to the people in front of them that their moving was not meant to be anti-social. The couple understood, and they struck up a conversation.

"Is that an accent you have? Where are you from?" Deanna asked.

"We have been living in St. Petersburg, Florida, for five years, but before that we lived in Russia," the woman responded.

"That is interesting," Deanna remarked. "My former mother-in-law also lived in St. Petersburg. Years ago she became very close to a family that had recently moved from Russia. They had lived in the same city as her family, prior to emigrating to the United States."

"How strange. We knew a woman whose family lived in the same city as us before we came to the United States. She was extremely kind to us, and we felt as though she were a member of our family. What was your mother-in-law's name?"

"Rose Shainberg," Deanna replied.

"I don't believe it! That was the lady!"

The foursome created quite a scene on the boat as they broke into tears and proceeded to hug each other.

Almost everyone in our family had met these people, except Deanna. Years earlier my wife and I accompanied Aunt Rose Shainberg in her attempt to locate the parents of this couple. We found them in an apartment in St. Petersburg, Florida, and despite our language barrier, there was an immediate connection. They had just arrived from Grodno, Russia. "Prior to the Second World War," they told us, "there had been over 30,000 Jews living in that community. The Nazis had murdered most of them, and recently there were only 13 remaining."

Rose Shainberg was a lifeline to this family as they struggled to adjust to their new home. She took them "under her wing" and saw to their needs. This act of kindness was typical of her. She spent her life looking for ways to help others. One day I asked her, "What inspired and motivated you to extend yourself so much?" She told me of the hardships her mother and siblings had endured as they traveled from Russia to America. There were five children with barely enough food. "At a train stop," her mother told her, "a group of women provided us with rolls and milk." That story had a great impact on Rose. She subsequently spent much of her life tangibly expressing her gratitude to those women by improving the lives of others. In 1984, she was honored as a recipient of the prestigious Eleanor Roosevelt Award *for a lifetime of humanitarian service.*

NEIGHBORS

Dr. Donald and Harriet Schaffer

Dr. Donald and Harriett Schaffer were visiting a former college friend in Mexico City. All were from Chicago, Illinois. The person they were visiting had a brother-in-law who operated a silver-plating business in Mexico City. Don expressed an interest in seeing the operation, and both agreed to come meet at the shop the following Tuesday. At the last minute, they were forced to change the day of their visit from Tuesday to Thursday. Prior to leaving, they were directed to a city bus; however, it proceeded to drop them off at the wrong place. They then hired a taxi driver who also failed to locate the factory. After wandering about for some time, they stumbled onto the right place. The owner, who was wrapping some items for a customer, asked them to wait until he was finished.

After striking up a conversation with the customer, Don commented on his accent.

"I'm from Australia," the man said.

"How interesting," replied Harriett. "The only people I know from Australia are my cousin Jack Crafty and his family, but I don't remember where they live."

"He is from Sydney," answered the gentleman, "and he happens to be my next door neighbor and best friend." He then proceeded to tell them about her family living in Australia. He was able to recite many stories of Harriett's family in the United States, stories he had heard from the Craftys over the years.

The Schaffers were stunned by the fact that their chances of meeting this man could have been thwarted had they kept their original meeting two days earlier, or had the bus and/or taxi found the factory earlier.

PINS ON A MAP

Harry Samuels

Returning from a trip in 1986 from Portland, Oregon, to Seattle, Washington, we decided to take a scenic side jaunt around Mt. St. Helen. We became lost in a rather isolated place. Spotting an A-frame structure in the woods, we met a forest ranger and proceeded to ask him for directions. He was sitting across from a makeshift board resting across two wooden sawhorses. He said he would be happy to direct us if we would first place a colored pin on a U.S. map that hung on the wall. Its purpose was to identify the places of origin of all the visitors.

As our traveling companion was inserting his pin, he turned to another visitor and said, "I'll bet you can't guess where I'm from."

"Where is that?" the lady asked.

"Jasper, Indiana," he exclaimed.

"Why, my son Joe is the Army recruiter there," she gasped. She was visibly shaken when told that her son and this stranger had eaten lunch together the previous Tuesday, and, moreover, that they were friends.

PARIS

Harry Samuels

On a trip to Paris, while standing in line with several hundred people to purchase tickets for the Eiffel Tower lift, I stood behind a traditionally dressed Pakistani couple. When we asked them where they were from, they replied, "New York." The gentleman said he was a pediatric oncologist doing research at a hospital in the city. I asked if he had ever heard of Dr. Blanche Alter who was in the same medical field and who also worked in a hospital in the city. "She is my boss," he replied.

Dr. Alter is a highly regarded and world-famous research scientist who kindly allowed us the use of her apartment in New York City in 1986 while she was traveling and our son was undergoing treatment at the Memorial Sloan-Kettering Cancer Center. We were deeply touched by her thoughtfulness and that of my cousin Adrianne Kelfer Wolf when they came to Memphis to see David and us in December 1987.

A MESSAGE

Harry Samuels

In December 2002, after returning from an 11,000-mile trip to Israel, Flora and I found a letter awaiting us at home. It had been mailed to us by our cousin Shelley Smuckler the same day we had embarked on our trip. While shopping for a birthday card, she had found it in a store in Bloomington, Indiana. Shelley was attracted to the card only because of the name on the front. It was misplaced in the card case since it was certainly not a birthday card. It was inserted upside down and above the compartment in which the other cards were properly located. In addition, it was not particularly eye-catching, having no bright colors, but rather containing dark blue and green shades. It read as follows:

You are

NEVER

Alone

And

Never

Will

You

BE   *David Samuels*

Inside, the card read: *I'm here for you.*

It is hard to believe that this was not a message from our beloved son who died in 1988 at age nineteen. He often spoke the words I'm here for you. *His name was David Samuels.*

I subsequently contacted the publishers of the card in order to locate their David Samuels. They told me that they had no record of anyone working for the company by that name.

THE TRAIN RIDE

Bernard Freiden

In 1985, Brad Freiden was to be married. His father Bernard Freiden drove his family to New York to attend the wedding. They spent the weekend in Far Rockaway and planned to drive to the city Sunday morning for the wedding ceremony. Brad mentioned that he had never traveled by train and asked if he and his dad might take the Long Island Railroad while Mrs. Freiden and other members of the family drove their car. They were no sooner seated on the train when a man approached and asked directions to a city in New Jersey. Bernard explained that he, too, was a stranger but advised the gentleman that someone at the train station would be able to help him.

Detecting an accent, Bernard asked his place of origin. He was told that he presently lived in Israel but formerly lived in Poland. He further explained that he had been in the printing business in Europe prior to the World War II, as had his father. Rolling up his sleeve, he showed Bernard the numbers tattooed on his arm, showing that he was a survivor of the Holocaust. "I was kept alive in Auschwitz only because I was helpful to the Nazis in printing counterfeit American twenty-dollar bills."

When asked his purpose in traveling to the United States, the man said that he had lost most of his family in the Holocaust and was now attempting to make contact with some relatives who might have remained in America. Showing Bernard and his son a list he had compiled of possible relatives in this country, he acknowledged that he had not yet located any of them. He added that he was not too optimistic about his prospects of finding anyone but wanted to make one final effort to do so.

Bernard wished him good luck in his quest and then introduced himself. The stranger said his name was Moishe Freidensohn. Bernard was shocked. He explained that when his father immigrated to the United States, his name also had been Freidensohn, subsequently shortened to Freiden. "I wonder if we are related," posed Bernard. "Why don't you check your list to see if it contains the name Yossel Freidensohn?" he suggested.

"I don't have to check," came the answer, "I am sure it is here."

"How can you be so sure?" inquired Bernard.

"Because he was my grandfather," replied Moishe.

"He was my grandfather, too," Bernard replied. "We are first cousins!"

Later, while visiting in Memphis, Moishe was introduced to some of the Holocaust survivors in the city. Among them was a Mr. Stefan Diament, operator of a printing business in Memphis. When they were introduced, Moishe made another surprising revelation. He explained that years earlier, his father had been helped in Poland by Jacob, Stefan's father. Both men had been in the printing business in Lodz before the war.

OUT OF AFRICA

Martin and Ruth Geller

Marty and Ruthie Geller attended a party on Long Island, New York, with eight other couples, some of whom were complete strangers. They played a game called "Six Degrees of Separation" in which participants would tell of unusual ways in which they or their friends had made connections with other people.

One of the couples, Sylvia and Morris Ostrow, mentioned that while traveling eight years earlier, they had crossed paths with George Levitt in the middle of Africa while they were on different safaris. When George learned they were all from cities on Long Island, he asked if they knew his good friend Marty Geller, his marine buddy during the Korean War. Everyone was impressed by the story, especially when it was acknowledged that the Gellers and the Ostrows had never met until that very evening at the party.

"But there is an addendum to this story," said Sylvia. Turning to Marty, she asked, "Do you and Ruth remember sitting in a restaurant in Spain eighteen years earlier? Next to you was a table with three college girls. You could tell from the conversation of the young ladies that they were obviously Americans and that they were very low in funds. As a thoughtful gesture and without mentioning what you were doing," she said to Marty, "you picked up their dinner check. When the girls walked to the cashier and learned their check had been paid, they asked the name of their benefactor."

That is how Sylvia and Morris first learned of the names Marty and Ruth Geller. One of the three girls in the restaurant that evening in Spain was the Ostrows' daughter.

Since meeting the Gellers eleven years ago, we have become very close. The act of kindness they extended to those girls in Spain reflects their character and personality. We feel blessed to know them.

THE PLAYER PIANO

Scott and Shay Poole

It was December 1, 2003, and we had just returned from a delightful weekend trip to Mountain View, Arkansas, where we stayed at a wonderful bed and breakfast facility called The Inn at Mountain View. Our hosts Scott and Shay Poole provided us with great accommodations, delicious food and outstanding music.

One morning at breakfast, a guest asked about an old player piano that graced their parlor. Scott began his response by acknowledging that his mother was descended from a family whose name was Busch. They were brewers who had come from Germany, married, and settled in St. Louis, Missouri. Scott's paternal grandparents gave the player piano to his parents. Scott recalled that he and his sister often played a game of drawing lines on the rolls of the music by connecting the holes that were punched in the paper. After their father died, Scott's mother moved to Little Rock and, in downsizing her home, felt compelled to sell the instrument.

Neither Scott nor his sister was particularly interested in music while growing up, but in later years they both exhibited some musical interest and talent. Scott plays the guitar, and his wife Shay plays the violin. Both of them are gifted musicians, and for years Scott had often voiced his regret over the loss of the instrument. On Thanksgiving Day 1998, a year after his mother's death, Scott and his wife visited his cousin in Dallas, Texas. During that holiday, he again expressed regret over the loss of the piano, and the families spent time that holiday lamenting its loss and expressing how much they wished it had remained in the family.

On their return trip to Cabot, Arkansas, the Pooles decided to make an unscheduled rest stop in Texarkana, Texas. They had recently made an offer to purchase a bed and breakfast facility in Mountain View, Arkansas. They were looking for old furnishings to put into their new place with the hope that their offer might be accepted. As they left their car, they spied an antique shop. Entering the store, they immediately noticed a player piano that closely resembled the one that their family had owned. Upon closer examination, Scott saw the marks he and his sister had made on it years earlier, and he immediately purchased the instrument. Shay was somewhat upset over the fact that they had just bought an object too large to be brought into their present house, but she says that she really couldn't fuss too much when she saw the tears of joy in her husband's eyes over the reunion. She just couldn't understand where they would keep it if their offer for the new lodge were not accepted within a reasonable time. The next morning, they received a call from the sellers of the inn and began the final negotiations leading to its purchase and the provision of a place of honor for the reclaimed piano.

One of the most memorable experiences of our trip occurred after we heard this story. When Scott told us that he was a member of the Busch beer clan from St. Louis, Missouri, I mentioned that I had once become friendly with a charming and beautiful girl there in the late 1940s, Patricia Busch. I had met her while working at a local downtown department store, Scruggs, Vandervort, and Barney, but I had lost track of her. "Could she possibly have been a member of your family?" Without another word, Scott left the room to retrieve a picture. It was of the girl I had remembered. As he showed it to me, he announced, "She was my mother."

VIENNA

Harry Samuels

It is May 2004, and we have just returned from a trip to Budapest, Vienna and Prague. Prior to our leaving, my friend Rabbi Levi Klein gave me the names and telephone numbers of Chabad Lubavitch rabbis in each city in the event we required assistance. Knowing the Chabad rabbis' reputation for hospitality, we were reluctant to contact them unnecessarily.

During our final day in Vienna, we purchased daily travel passes, allowing us to use all forms of the city's excellent transportation system. We planned to get lost exploring the city by bus, tram and metro. It was then that an unforgettable experience occurred.

While riding on a city bus along the shore of the Danube River, we decided to try to find the synagogue of the three rabbis in Vienna whose names had been given to me in Memphis. We wished to get an indication of what it was like to live within a small Jewish community in a city of 1,700,000, one that had been the former home of Adolph Hitler. We asked numerous individuals throughout the city for directions to the synagogue but were consistently told we were miles away from the area.

As we passed several bridges on our right, I said that for some reason, I felt drawn to an area at the end of a bridge across a ravine. Our companions Lennie and Louise Newman were convinced that the Jewish area was several miles south along the Danube River, but they followed us from the bus. Crossing the bridge, we came to a fork in the street. With no hesitation we took the left one and proceeded only a few yards when we met an elderly woman who seemed to understand my Yiddish-German. I asked if she knew of a synagogue in the area. Before she responded, a small group of men walked toward us. They had overheard my attempt to speak Yiddish. From their attire it was obvious that they were Jewish. They were walking home, following morning religious services. I asked if they knew Rabbis Biederman, Edelman, or Gruzman. One of them replied, "Two of those men are standing before you."

Approximately one hundred yards from where we stood were four white pillars, extending perhaps eighty feet into the air. They were arranged in an arc and stood approximately ten feet apart. Since they supported nothing, it seemed apparent they comprised a monument of some sort. A metal plaque was attached to a gate nearby. On it was sketched the outline of the former synagogue that had stood there, one that was destroyed by the Nazis during "Kristlenacht," 1938. Apparently the four pillars represented the four corners of that building.

Beyond the gate, partially rebuilt, was the synagogue we had been seeking.

Had we not come at that very moment, this story might never have been written. Some day I hope to understand the purpose that was served by this experience. It was certainly synchronistic and a little spooky.

BRITISH FRIENDS

Harry Samuels

While on a trip to Florence, Italy, in 1994, Flora and I met Rex and Carol Kilby, a lovely couple from Windsor, England. It was a beautiful day, and they were seated beside us at lunch outside a *trattoria* near the Uffizi Museum. Nearby stood the magnificent replica of the statue of Michelangelo's *David*. My wife and I were having difficulty explaining our wishes to a waiter when Rex offered to help. A few words in Italian from him solved our problem. We chatted a few minutes before leaving the restaurant to explore some nearby shops. A short time later, I saw them in the plaza. "There is the couple we just met," I told my wife. "They seem to be rushing toward us." They breathlessly handed us a card listing their home address and telephone number, with the request that we contact them the next time we were in England. They told us that they enjoyed our short visit so much that they wished to spend more time with us and to show us a part of their country. I took their photograph, and sending it to them began a correspondence that has lasted. A couple of years later, having come to London for a short visit, we invited them for lunch. They insisted on showing us Blenheim Palace and the city of Oxford; they ended the day taking us to a 600-year-old pub for dinner.

Two years later we learned that they were planning a trip to America and convinced them to spend a week with us in Memphis. We showed them some of the sights of our city, including several of the facilities where we volunteered. We took them to the Ronald McDonald House—"The House That Love Built." It provides housing for patients and their families coming to the St. Jude Children's Research Hospital for treatment.

During our final breakfast together, I noticed a white envelope. Rex remarked, "We know you would not allow us to reimburse you for our expenses, but we want you to donate this money to your favorite charity." My wife replied, "We are most appreciative of this gesture, but it would be more appropriate for you to donate the funds to a charity in England in our honor." A few weeks later, we received a letter from the Ronald McDonald House in London attesting to the donation. Included in the letter was a picture of our friends taken at that facility where they had become volunteers.

While at the Ronald McDonald House, we introduced our guests Rex and Carol Kilby to Rick and Carol Kirby—no easy task considering the similarity of their names. Carol Kirby was the executive director of the facility. Since that time, the Kirbys have visited the Kilbys in England and have become friends. That lunch in Florence has led to numerous connections.

PART V
A MIXTURE

CHANUKAH GIFT

Rabbi Moishe Bryski

One winter day, a group of rabbinical students came from New York to Agoura, California, to assist the rabbi of the Chabad Congregation. It was a Saturday when a moving truck began unloading next to the home in which the boys were housed. Although it was the Sabbath—a day of rest, prayer, and reflection for observant Jews—the young men were eager to extend hospitality to their new neighbors. They were told the newcomers were a man and his daughter. He had been hired as the music conductor and choir leader of a reform temple in the valley. The young men observed the rituals of the Sabbath, whereas the lifestyles of the man and his daughter were far removed from those of a traditional Jewish family. Yet the newcomers were immediately and wholeheartedly welcomed by the young men with food, Sabbath songs, and open arms.

As time progressed, the newcomers became more comfortable in their new environment. The choir leader decided one evening to attend a class conducted by Rabbi Moishe Bryski, the Agoura Chabad rabbi. The subject of the rabbi's talk was "Faith and Suffering." Following the lecture, he came to the rabbi, hugged him, and, filled with emotion, proceeded to cry on his shoulder as he related this story. A year before moving to Agoura, he had lost his wife and two of his three children in a terrible automobile accident. At that time he was so distraught that he gave up. He couldn't fight the pain or cope with the loss. He was angry at G-d, and he hated the thought of living. It was then he decided he wanted to die. He planned to take his surviving daughter to the movies, to spend one last night with her, and afterwards to take her home and commit suicide while she was asleep. The two went to the Mountain Gate Plaza Cinema in Simi Valley, and as they came into the mall, they heard the sound of Jewish music. It was Chanukah, and some group was having a Chanukah festival in front of the theater. They were distracted as they watched the dancing and listened to the music. Soon he and his daughter were invited to join in the dancing. There he was, the same night that he had decided to end his life, dancing with his daughter. He knew at that moment that he would not give up on life but try again. He decided to find another community and start a new life, and he asked G-d to send him a sign that He was there watching over him. The next thing he knew, he and his daughter were being welcomed by the local Chabad rabbi and his rabbinic students in Agoura.

Rabbi Bryski listened to the man's story, and suddenly he, too, was crying. He asked him to wait a few minutes while he ran to his office and rummaged through some albums taken at Simi during the previous Chanukah. There it was in a photo. It was they, the rabbi and his Chabad group, who were there at the mall that night. That was the year the rabbi had decided to add another city to their list of Chanukah festivals. Why Simi? Why Mountain Gate? He didn't know. Why did they grab a total stranger and ask him to dance? Why not? It was Chanukah, and their injunction from the Rebbe was to bring the joy and message of Chanukah to all, so that everyone should know that light will prevail over darkness. So they did, and there it was in the album, a photo of the man and his daughter dancing with the Chabad group.

Recalling that night several years later, the rabbi remembered his wife's concerns about the size of the crowd and the effectiveness of that program at Simi. He remembered that he, too, had questioned its success in his own mind. Was the crowd adequate? Did it justify all the extra effort? Was it really worthwhile? He never dreamt that it might have helped to save a person's life.

The good deeds we perform can have a ripple effect far beyond our ability to imagine.

ABALONE

Bernard Kivowitz

Bernie Kivowitz arrived late in San Francisco, California, and decided he would eat abalone, his favorite dish, for dinner. He was staying at a hotel near the airport, but the concierge sent him to a small restaurant in a remote spot of the Bay Area, some distance away, for the treat.

While waiting for his meal, a teenage girl walked by his table. She resembled the daughter of his next-door neighbors of long ago, the Shells, in Roseland, New Jersey. He followed her to her table to determine if his hunch could be correct. When her mother Pat Shell saw him, she gasped.

He thought her reaction peculiar until she explained that someone that very day had called to advise that a former next-door neighbor in Roseland had died. She had assumed it was Bernie.

OSCAR

Harry Samuels

One spring evening four years ago, a small, dark wren perched on the extremely narrow ledge of trim above the front entry of our house. It was only a guess, but we assumed it to be a male, so we named him "Oscar." It placed its wings over its head and remained in that position until daybreak the next day. For two months this routine was repeated nightly. We never fed or encouraged him, but we became quite attached to the little bird. He had become a part of our family, notwithstanding the problem his presence created. We felt compelled to use only our garage door while entering and leaving the house in the evening since we didn't want to disturb him while he was perched.

When the weather turned cool, he left. The next spring he returned again to the same spot over our front door. The following spring he failed to return, and we missed him. One day I told our next door neighbor that we really missed Oscar and that we feared something must have happened to him. That very evening he returned.

Can people have synchronistic experiences with animals? We did!

SHIVA

Murray Habbaz

During the late 1940s, Ralph Habbaz lived in Brooklyn with his wife Mary, his daughter Rennee, and his son Murray. Ralph's physician insisted that he remain at home for a minimum of two weeks following surgery. His elderly mother, who lived nearby, came each day to prepare meals for her son while everyone else was working or at school. Following a week of inactivity, Ralph announced that he felt better and thought he would return to work early, contrary to his doctor's instructions. "Better I should die and you should be forced to stay home *sitting shiva for me*," his mother exclaimed. (Upon the death of a parent, most Jews observe seven days of mourning, remaining in their homes while close family members and friends visit the bereaved and participate in prayer services held there. The word *shiva* means *seven* in Hebrew.) Two days later her words appeared prescient when she was found dead in her bed. Her son was then obligated to remain home by the stricture of his tradition.

During the following week, Murray felt confined, staying in their apartment day and night. One day he walked outside and onto the upstairs landing. (They lived on the second floor of a two-unit flat.) There he saw a man dressed in a white suit, standing alone. He asked if he could be of help, and the man replied that he was hungry. The Habbaz family invited him into their apartment, giving him a meal and a few dollars. As the man started to leave, there was an audible groan from the adjoining bedroom. It was Murray's mother Mary who suffered from terrible headaches. The man asked if he might see her, and when he was taken into her bedroom, he placed his hands upon her head. Immediately, she felt relief.

As the stranger left the apartment, Ralph directed his son Murray to bring him back. He wanted to give him some additional money. Murray ran to the stairway, the only entrance and exit from the apartment, but the man had left. He called to his sister who was sitting at the entry of the building downstairs and asked her to tell the man to return. She said that she had been there for the past thirty minutes, and no one had entered or left during that time.

THE DREAM

Naava Parker

During September of last year, she thought she had detected an extremely slight change in her breast, prompting her to undergo a digital mammogram and ultrasound examination. The doctor was pleased to advise her that everything looked clean.

But from October until January, she began to experience disturbing dreams almost every night. In those dreams, a number of deceased family members kept appearing and insisting that she did have cancer and that she must have it removed. Her concerns led her to seek a second opinion; however, that physician, too, said he could find no evidence of cancer in her body. As the dreams continued, she met with a third doctor who said he believed she did have cancer. He based his belief on a slight difference in her skin appearance and the constant dreams she was experiencing. This doctor sent her to a surgeon who planned a lumpectomy at a specific site on her breast. Neither she nor her husband had positive feelings toward that surgeon, so they sought another opinion. The last doctor who examined her selected a different spot for the biopsy from the one planned by the previous physician. Afterwards, an analysis of the tissue determined that her breast was definitely cancerous and that it required a mastectomy, chemotherapy, and radiation. When the entire tissue was examined, it was found that the only area that was cancer free was the exact spot her previous doctor had planned for a biopsy.

Though interesting and thought provoking, how does this experience relate to synchronicity? Clearly, we have special connections with those who have preceded us.

The patient intends to write a manual based on her experiences as well as the experiences of others. It is to be written from the perspective of one who has been diagnosed with breast cancer. She intends to include information that she and others have found helpful in the hopes of assisting current and future patients.

THE MOVIE

Dr. Bryan Rigg

Dr. Bryan Rigg is the product of a protestant Texas family. In 1992, while enrolled at Yale University, he decided to spend some time in Berlin exploring his family's roots; at the same time, he was becoming more proficient in German. A teacher at the Goethe Institute of Berlin suggested he see the movie *Europa, Europa* to help him become more comfortable with the language. The movie is about a man of Jewish descent who hid his religious background while serving in the German army. There was only one other person in the theater that evening, Peter Millies, an elderly German gentleman who was fluent in English as well as German. He kindly proceeded to help translate the movie for Bryan. After the movie, while they enjoyed a drink together, Mr. Millies acknowledged that he, too, had been able to hide his own Jewish ethnicity. He said that he had served in the Wermacht during World War II, just as the protagonist in the movie.

Bryan was intrigued by the fact that there were German men of Jewish descent who had served in Hitler's army. It triggered a study that continued until he had obtained 430 personal interviews and 30,000 pages of testimony. He subsequently developed this mass of material into a best-selling book, *Hitler's Jewish Soldiers: The Untold Story of Nazi Racial Laws and Men of Jewish Descent in the German Military.*

What began as a suggestion to spend an evening at the movies made a significant impact on the life of the author. It has resulted in a fascinating and unique historical document that brought to light a hitherto obscure and practically forgotten story of those tragic times.

Dr. Bryan Mark Rigg is a remarkable man. Overcoming perceptual handicaps as a child that caused him to fail the first grade, he subsequently received a B.A. degree with honors in history from Yale University and an M.A. degree and a Ph.D. from Cambridge. He served as an officer in the U.S. Marine Corps and as a volunteer in the Israeli army. He has engaged in extensive humanitarian work in Romania, Bulgaria, the Bahamas, South Africa, and France. He helped develop a church network that cares for children and adults, has helped build a church, and has worked as a mime. He is currently a professor of history at the American Military University.

THE EAGLE SCOUT

Stephen Posner

Marvin and Shirley Posner invited us for dinner that Sunday. We arrived a little early and were sitting on the front porch that afternoon when their son Steve returned home from a camping trip with the Boy Scouts. Shirley, his mother, hadn't been too keen on his participating since doctors had told her to restrict his physical activities. (He was still recuperating from surgery and chemotherapy necessitated by a serious tumor that had manifested itself in his leg.) He was a dutiful son but fortunately was insistent on making the trip that day. Although the doctors hadn't ruled out swimming, his weak leg didn't offer much assistance, and this weakness prevented him from becoming a strong swimmer capable of obtaining the life-saving merit badge. That badge was required in order for him to achieve his goal of becoming an Eagle Scout.

When Steve came home, we noticed his wrinkled uniform and his disheveled appearance. He said *hello* to everyone and immediately went to his bedroom without discussing his trip. A few minutes later, the telephone rang and Shirley spoke with the wife of one of the adults who had accompanied the scouts that day. Shirley explained that the lady had called to express her thanks to Steve for having saved her husband's life after his boat sank. Steve remembered that one of the adults was unable to swim, and the man had failed to wear a life jacket that day. He proceeded to stuff life preservers under him and helped bring him to safety. Steve had always been a modest individual, though gifted with a keen, dry sense of humor, and he did not mention the incident to anyone. It was just something that had to be done, and he did it. When the news of his achievement was made public, he received a letter of commendation from the National Boy Scouts Council. They decided that he had earned his life-saving merit badge—the hard way.

REDEMPTION

Harry Samuels

My uncle William Samuels was one of those rare individuals whose very presence made the world seem brighter. During the 1960s, he and his wife Fannie lived in Paragould, Arkansas. Often they spent the night at our apartment prior to leaving from the Memphis airport. They would often bring "trip" gifts for us. Once, upon returning from a jaunt to Las Vegas, Uncle Willie handed my wife five silver dollars as a souvenir. She placed them in a drawer and soon forgot about them. In 1965, we discovered we were expecting a child. Before our son was born, Uncle Willie died.

Pursuant to Jewish tradition, one month after the birth of a first son, it is mandated to have a religious ceremony. At that time, the child is symbolically redeemed by a *kohen*, or descendent of the priestly caste, for five silver coins. This redemptive service is done in accordance with the biblical injunction mandating that first-born male children were to be taken to the holy temple to serve G-d unless redeemed from the priests. But in the 1960s, it was not easy to obtain silver dollars since many had long since become collectors' items. It was then that Flora remembered her old gift, and she retrieved the coins given her years earlier by Uncle Willie. These we used to "redeem" our son, whom we appropriately named William Samuels.

THE SPIRITUALIST

Irma Sheon

Several years ago, a member of our family came to Memphis to attend a funeral. She told us that prior to her marriage, she had visited a spiritualist in the Washington, D.C., area who had been highly recommended. He told her that she was going to marry a tall, dark-haired young man by the name of David and that they would have twins, although she would not be their birth mother.

Time passed, and she did meet and marry David, only to learn that she was suffering from a serious ailment requiring surgery. This operation would preclude her from ever bearing children. She and her husband decided to harvest some of her eggs prior to surgery in the hopes of finding a surrogate mother.

One day they received a call from an attorney who knew of their situation and had received a call from a married woman with several children of her own. The woman wished to be a surrogate mother and thereby enable a childless couple to experience the pleasures of parenthood. My twin cousins came to join our family in this special way.

Apparently some people have the ability to connect to future events!

THE LORD AND THE LADY

Harry Samuels

Unfortunately, we are not always capable of appreciating the examples of syn-chronicity we experience at the time, and we often fail to view them in a positive manner due to our limited means of evaluation at the time. Sometimes we are fortunate to be able to see not only pieces of the puzzle fitting together but also the overall design of the puzzle that affirms purpose.

A number of years ago, my wife and I attended a lecture at the Memphis Jew-ish Community Center presented by a world-famous author Rabbi Immanuel Jakobovitz, of blessed memory. He spoke on the topic "Jewish Medical Ethics," a term he himself had coined. Years earlier he had written one of the definitive books on the subject. He had just finished serving as chief rabbi of Great Britain and had been the first chief rabbi in the history of the British Empire to be inducted into the House of Lords. Following his remarks, several people in the audience approached him. They all wished to obtain autographed copies of his books. Usually we enjoy meeting visiting dignitaries such as the rabbi, but with so many people around him, we opted to leave. At that moment the executive director of the Jewish Community Center, Mr. Barrie Weiser, asked if we would be willing to host the two of them for lunch the following day. We were delighted to do so, and as a result were able to spend a wonderful few hours with them at our home, learning of their most interesting lives and past experiences. One such experience dealt with his investiture as a member of the House of Lords; another was of their subsequent visit with the Royal Family at Windsor Castle.

They told us that everyone dresses formally for dinner at Windsor. The queen was very considerate and did not hesitate to provide kosher food for all of her guests during that visit.

The Lord and the Lady were assigned adjoining bedrooms. While dressing, Rabbi Jakobovitz noticed that all of the money, queen's face upward, had been removed from his trousers and placed upon his dresser. Fluffed around his wife's peignoir and gown was her husband's *tallit*, or prayer shawl. It was in a velvet bag, and the castle staff—unfamiliar with guests using it for prayers each morning—assumed it to be her evening shawl!

Following our lunch, my wife accompanied Lady J, as she was called, on a shopping trip while I took her husband to the Memphis Jewish Community Center to swim. During their time together, Lady J, a most charming and bright individual with whom Flora and I both fell in love, asked my wife about our children, one of whom had died at age nineteen of a rare malignancy. Flora told her that we had subsequently established a multi-faceted social support system in his memory called *Chai,* meaning *life* in Hebrew. It was designed to help families whose children were suffering catastrophic illnesses. Lady J. seemed quite surprised, remarking that six months earlier a child of her close friend in England had died. She, too, had established a multi-faceted social support system in Great Britain in memory of her friend's child, and she, too, had named it *Chai.*

A week later we received a call from Rabbi and Mrs. Maurice Lamm in California with whom the Jakobovitzes had visited after leaving Memphis. They had told the Lamms of our *Chai* group in Memphis. The Lamms were in the process of developing a National Jewish Hospice organization, and they began sending us material about it with the understanding that we would send them information about *Chai.* We were unfamiliar with hospice prior to that time but were quickly intrigued by what we learned. We began an investigation of the program, resulting in our becoming volunteers with the local Methodist Alliance Hospice; we subsequently made connections with other hospice groups in the city.

Ultimately we helped establish a Jewish Hospice initiative, training fifty-three volunteers for service with all the major hospices in Memphis. A few years later in England, we were able to visit Dame Cicely Saunders, the founder of the modern worldwide hospice movement. She was extremely hospitable to us and mentioned that Rabbi Lord Jakobovitz was a valued member of her board of directors.

Many lives have been touched as a result of a chance meeting with strangers. Or was it "chance"? I prefer to think otherwise. I believe it was the hand of our son David that guided us to an expansion of hospice in Memphis, something he would have wanted to do.

In the late 1940s, Mrs. Cicely Saunders served as a medical social worker at St. Thomas, a London hospital. One of her patients was a forty-year-old Polish man named David Tasma who was terminally ill. During the course of their conversations, he expressed the hope that someday there would be a facility for the treatment of the terminally ill where patients would be treated with palliative care rather than aggressive medicine. He wanted a place in which patients could be visited any time of the day or night and even be permitted to have their pets visit. To that end, prior to his death, Mr. Tasma made arrangements to leave his modest estate in her care with the wish: "I would be a window in your home."

After completing her medical school education and receiving her degree, Dr. Saunders spent seven years studying pain management. She feels this was her major contribution in helping to make possible the establishment of the modern hospice movement, allowing patients to die in their own homes.

In 1967, St. Christopher's was dedicated as the world's first modern residential hospice. It is situated in Sydenham, a small village south of London. At the base of a large picture window near the front entry, there is a plaque that reads: *I will be a window in your home, the promise of David Tasma of Warsaw, who died 25 February 1948, and who made the first gift to St. Christopher's.*

Dr. Saunders has been referred to as a modern-day Florence Nightingale and has already greatly improved the final days of millions of people around the world. Although she was bestowed the title *Dame of the British Empire* for her achievements, she is quite modest and reluctant even to have her picture taken. On a recent visit to the portrait gallery in London, I spoke with its twentieth-century curator and noted that there was a national treasure missing from the gallery, namely Dame Cicely. The curator replied that the staff had tried unsuccessfully several times to obtain her permission for a portrait that might be displayed with other British notables' portraits and that she and her staff would be most appreciative if I could help them obtain one.

CARACAS

Rabbi Levi Klein

A few years ago, my friend, Rabbi Levi Klein of Memphis, met and became friendly with Dr. Eli Benaim, a pediatric oncologist from Caracas, Venezuela; Dr. Benaim had recently joined the staff of St. Jude Children's Research Hospital in Memphis. The rabbi mentioned that he had spent two years working in Caracas and remembered having met Dr. Benaim's grandfather there.

After he displayed a photo album of his sojourn, the two reviewed issues of a newspaper Rabbi Klein had kept as souvenirs. Examining them, they were riveted to the back page of one of the papers, the entirety of which contained the obituary of Dr. Benaim's father.

Rabbi Klein is the spiritual leader of the Chabad Lubavitch Congregation of Memphis. He serves not only the needs of his congregants but of prisoners in three states, in addition to Jewish families who bring their children to St. Jude's for treatment. His father Rabbi Binyomin Klein was a personal secretary of the last Lubavitcher Rebbe. He was the son of the late Rabbi Menachem Klein who served during the last century as head of the Chevra Kiddusha *or Holy Society of Jerusalem. That group continues to serve as the Jewish burial society of the city and as the provider of acts of loving-kindness.*

THE COINS

Rabbi Leivi Sudak

Last year a friend told of his four-year-old nephew who, while living with his parents in London, ran into the street and was hit by a car. While the ambulance drove them to the emergency room, the child's mother and one attendant remained in the rear of the ambulance with the little boy while the father, a rabbi, rode with the driver. Upon arriving at the hospital, the attendants immediately rushed the patient into the building.

As he left the ambulance, the father noticed a partially finished Coke wedged next to the driver's seat, and in order to provide the two medics with drinks they had missed, he placed two one-pound coins on the dashboard. It was subsequently determined that the child was not severely injured, and the following day he was released from the hospital.

A week later, while attending the Friday evening service at his synagogue, a member of the congregation asked the rabbi if his son had recently been injured. When he acknowledged the fact, the man asked if he had left coins on the dashboard of the ambulance. Affirming that he had done so, the man reminded the rabbi of an episode that had occurred eighteen months earlier when the congregant's niece had married a non-Jewish man.

"The woman had subsequently given birth to a son, but the father had refused to allow the child to be circumcised in accordance with Jewish law. Months later, the father had reluctantly allowed the ceremony to take place, but during that afternoon something seemed wrong. The baby's mother called you to come quickly to see the child, and you raced across London to solve the problem."

Having been reminded of the experience, the rabbi asked what the incident had to do with the present story. The man explained that the baby's father was the ambulance driver. When he returned to the vehicle that day and saw the coins, he was very touched by the gesture made at such a stressful moment. He wished to learn more of a religion that helped develop such character in people; he subsequently decided to convert to Judaism.

Even a small gesture can have a great impact.

MEALS ON WHEELS

Leonard and Louise Newman

My cousins, Leonard and Louise Newman, called a year ago to say the Friends of the School of Music at the Indiana University, one of the finest music schools in the world, had just received a large bequest. Louise was the president of the "Friends" and was apprised of the bequest by the dean of the school. He asked her to sign the necessary papers establishing the endowment. It was the largest bequest the "Friends" had received to date. They had difficulty identifying the donor until the Newmans recalled that she had been a recipient of the Meals on Wheels they had delivered over the years.

It seems that their routine was for Lennie to drive while Louise delivered. She acknowledged that she spent very little time visiting since she was intent on insuring that all the recipients received hot meals. Onc day Lennie delivered the food and met the recipient. She asked about Len's wife. He replied that she was working to raise some money in order to provide scholarships for needy students. Evidently that information played a role in the bequest.

I am proud of the fact that I introduced Lennie and Louise to each other fifty-four years ago. They have been happily married these past fifty-three years and continue to be a blessing to all those who know them and to many who do not. Since retiring from business in Jasper, Indiana, they have become outstanding supporters of Indiana University's School of Music. They entertain the residents of a local nursing home by playing the piano and the accordion. He is the volunteer chairman of the local SCORE office, serving the needs of aspiring business owners.

THE YAHRZEIT LIGHT

Rabbi Levi Klein

It is traditional for Jewish people to light a memorial candle on the anniversary of the death of a loved one. And so it was earlier last year that Rabbi Klein, head of Chabad Lubavitch of Tennessee Congregation (See "Caracas," p.85.) lit a candle in Memphis on the anniversary of the death of a friend and former member of his congregation, Steve Lipson. Within moments of lighting the candle, the rabbi received a telephone call from his wife Rifka Klein who was attending a conference in New York for wives of Chabad rabbis. She mentioned that something interesting had just occurred when another attendee, Mrs. Brackman, approached her with a remarkable story.

Mrs. Brackman and her husband Rabbi Yossi Brackman operate a Chabad Center at the University of Chicago. In order to attract students, they invited a well-known and highly regarded economics professor, Dr. Charles Lipson, to deliver a talk the previous Friday evening following the religious service. Those who knew of the professor discouraged the effort, saying that he was in such great demand he was seldom able to accept local speaking engagements. Mrs. Brackman persisted, and to the delight of all, the request was granted. The speaker prefaced his remarks by saying that since it was the first anniversary of his brother's death, he wished to dedicate his talk to Steve's memory and to the Chabad rabbi and his wife in Memphis, Tennessee, who had befriended him—the Kleins.

Why did the call from Rabbi Klein's wife come within only a minute of his lighting the memorial candle? What caused Mrs. Brackman to approach Mrs. Klein at that very same time? They all seemed to be on a similar wavelength. How often have you placed a telephone call to someone only to have that person tell you that he or she was getting ready to call you or was thinking of you that very moment?

We subsequently learned that Mrs. Brackman is the grandaughter of our close friends, Marty and Laverne("Tootie") Hecht, from Cape Girardeau, Missouri.(See "Jerusalem" p.38.)

YANKEE TALK

May Lynn Mansbach

In 1993, the parents of the groom were in the process of planning a wedding in New Jersey. Wanting to make it special for the groom's family, who were from the North, May Lynn and her husband Charles decided to prepare two lists of words or phrases to give to each guest: one listing *How to Speak Northern*, the other, *How to Speak Southern*. Living in Memphis at that time, it was not difficult for them to create the "Southern Talk" list. However, finding things to write for "Yankee Talk" posed a problem. They called the local library and bookstores but had no success. Next, they contacted the New York City Public Library and even the Library of Congress, but they were of no help. Finally they became reconciled to the fact that they were not going to be able to create two lists and decided to print only the "southern" one.

May Lynn first visited a local printer and rejected his proposal, but that stop proved to be a significant one since it delayed her twenty minutes. She then took the list to Kinko's where she waited patiently behind another customer. As the gentleman in front of her handed his papers to the clerk for processing, she noticed a book he was holding in his hand entitled *Northern Talk*. Startled, she told him of their experience, and the man happily allowed her to borrow his book.

Not only was May Lynn thoughtful in sharing this delightful story, but she has made very helpful suggestions for this manuscript. She and her husband, Dr. Charles Mansbach, are wonderful friends and good tennis players.

EDEN ALTERNATIVE

Harry Samuels

The Introduction mentions that the death of our son (David Samuels) allowed us to create some very special connections with a number of attendant but unanticipated results. One of them (See "The Lord and the Lady," p.82) led to an expansion of local hospice programs. This one deals with the establishment of the Eden Alternative in the Memphis Jewish Nursing Home.

The story began six years ago when Mr. Danny Siegel, a prolific author known as "The Mitzvah Man," called to alert our community about Mrs. Susan Lyon and her three-year-old daughter Alyssa from North Potomac, Maryland. "The Lyons are flying to Memphis," he said, "for treatment at St. Jude Children's Research Hospital. Alyssa is suffering from a brain tumor, and her family has no one in the city to lend support during this stressful time." Following the death of our son, we had become volunteers at the Ronald McDonald House, and I had become a member of its local board. That magnificent institution provides housing and additional support for patients and their families coming to St. Jude. It was *beshert* that we were called. From that time until the present, my wife and I have felt we were abundantly blessed to have begun this relationship, one that has continued to grow over the years. We feel that we are the adoptive parents and grandparents of the beautiful Lyon family.

A year later I wrote a letter to Mr. Danny Siegel, thanking him for introducing our community to the Lyons, and I enclosed a modest check payable to his Ziv Tzedakah Fund.* He acknowledged the donation and enclosed a copy of the fund's annual report. It lists all of the recipients, the amount each agency received, and the purpose of each organization. Looking at the brochure, I noticed that he had given some money to a nursing home for the purchase of a birdcage. He added, "If you would like to know how life can be made worthwhile in a nursing home, read the book *Life Worth Living* by Dr. William H. Thomas. "

As a board member of the Memphis Jewish Home, a 144-bed nursing facility, I was intrigued by Dr. Thomas's concept, which he termed *The Eden Alternative.* Armed with a copy of his book and much enthusiasm, I visited the director of the nursing home in order to induce him to consider adopting the program. He was about to retire and, understandably, was not eager to start anything so new and revolutionary. His successor, too, was not initially excited about the idea of increasing his workload and that of his associates; however, after he and some of his board members (and former board presidents) read *Life Worth Living*, things began to materialize. Following a thorough study and evaluation, the facility became the first nursing home in the state of Tennessee to become *Edenized*.

My wife and I believe we have acted as shaliachs, *or messengers, of our son in this matter. As a young boy, he expressed the wish to be able someday to give back to society some of the blessings he had received. Even now he seems to be realizing his wish.*

In his book Life Worth Living, *Dr. Thomas writes of the three plagues that afflict residents of nursing homes: helplessness, loneliness, and boredom. He recites numerous ways in which these evils might be addressed with the Eden Alternative, such as through the empowerment of personnel, the introduction of plants and animals into the residence, and inter-generational participation. Dr. Thomas is one of the most caring individuals I have ever met. At last count, his Eden process had been incorporated into 284 nursing homes throughout the United States.*

*The Ziv Tzedakah Fund is a non-profit fund established by Danny Siegel. It provides money and support for individuals and programs that offer direct, significant, and immediate services to the needy with a minimum of overhead and bureaucracy. He has collected and distributed funds to dozens of worthy causes, ranging from a food program in Philadelphia for homeless people to a lady in Israel who collects used wedding dresses for poor brides.
(For more information, contact the Ziv Tzedakah Fund, 384 Wyoming Avenue, Millburn, NJ 07040.)

THE DINNER GUEST

Sydney and Marilyn Pollack

Among the twelve dinner guests seated at the table of friends in Memphis, Tennessee, were Sydney and Marilyn Pollack. After the meal they approached another guest, a young physician from Israel.

"Do you know anyone from Israel?" the young visitor inquired.

"Only two couples we met there last year," replied Sydney. "One couple who is related to our brother-in-law was very hospitable."

Marilyn added, "They held a party in our honor and invited some friends to meet us. They showed us photographs of their family and wedding pictures of their daughter, who had recently been married. This may sound strange," she declared, "but one of those people in that album resembled you."

"What were the names of your hosts?" asked the young man.

"Dalia and Rafi Meshullam," said Sydney. "Do you know them?"

"I married their daughter. The picture you saw was of *me!*"

FROM CAPE TO THE NEGEV

Harry Samuels

When my father died in 1940, I was nine years old. Since we lived in Cape Girardeau, Missouri, at that time, we couldn't depend on having enough Jewish men to recite the *kaddish*, the memorial prayer, on the anniversary of his death. (Ten men are required.) I, therefore, traveled to St. Louis, Missouri, to attend services at a synagogue, Tiferes Israel Congregation. It was there that I met Rabbi Yeheschal Hartman, of blessed memory.

During the years that followed that meeting, Rabbi Hartman moved to Israel and became a professor of sociology at Bar Ilan University. But our paths continued to cross when he came to visit his brother Rabbi Eli Hartman, who had moved to Memphis to direct a Jewish orthodox day school. Additionally, I had become acquainted with another brother, Rabbi Dr. David Hartman, an internationally known scholar who is considered by many to be the recognized leader of the modern orthodox movement. He established the Shalom Hartman Institute in Jerusalem.

One day during the 1960s, I received a frantic telephone call from a local friend, telling me that his young teenage nephew had fallen prey to a cult group living in the Negev desert near Be'er-Sheva, Israel. The family was desperate to extricate their son from the clutches of those people, but they didn't know how to go about the task. Remembering my old friend Yeheschal who lived in Tel-Aviv, I called to tell him of the situation. He immediately drove into the desert and brought the young man home to his grateful family.

Maybe my travel to St. Louis to recite the kaddish was beshert, *providing a link to that young man in the desert.*

While attending a biennial assembly of the Jewish Community Center Association in St. Louis, I met Rabbi Donniel Hartman, a highly regarded scholar and charming individual who is currently the director of the Hartman Institute and the son of Rabbi David Hartman. I told him of some of the connections I had made with members of his family over the years and that his Uncle Yeheschal had been a good friend. He told me that he, too, had been very fond of his uncle, and he shared some interesting information. When his aunt and uncle were still living in St. Louis, they became quite close to a dentist and his wife who were stationed at a nearby Army base. They were such good friends that they decided to give their daughter the same name as the daughter of Uncle Yeheschal. And that is how Donniel came to marry a girl named after his own grandmother!

THE SINGER

Shuli Natan

It is April 2004, and we have just dined with several Memphis couples and with Mrs. Shuli Natan, perhaps the most famous singer in Israel. When asked how her career developed, she told us that as a youngster she had appeared once on an afternoon radio program featuring young talents. It was 1967, and it was the only radio station in the country at that time. Listening to the program that afternoon was an accomplished songwriter, Naomi Shemer, and her daughter. Naomi had just written a song: It was to serve as a tribute to the city of Jerusalem at the Israel Independence Day song festival celebration. She was so impressed by the young voice that she jotted down her name and asked her daughter to place it in a drawer. She was already sure she wanted her to be the one to introduce her new song, even though they had never met. The producers of the song festival felt that only a professional should present the song, but they capitulated when Naomi told them that it would be Shuli or no one.

The song "Jerusalem of Gold" was an instant success. It was selected as the most popular song in the country and helped establish the outstanding career of a young teenager.

While reviewing this story for the last time, I learned of the death of Naomi Shemer. Her songs will never die.

THE SPILL

Tova Mirvis

A most compassionate, perceptive, and imaginative young writer—and a favorite of mine—is Tova Mirvis. Her best selling book *The Ladies Auxiliary* has received tremendous acclaim. Its message is so universal that it has been reprinted in other languages. It was written in a corner of a Starbucks Coffee Shop in New York City approximately two years ago. She did not plan another book so soon, but for the past two years she has felt another story was waiting to be told.

At her parents' home in Memphis last month, she told us about the progression of writing her second book. She said that although she had worked diligently, "It just wasn't going anywhere." Again she was writing at a Starbucks in New York when she accidentally spilled a cup of coffee on her computer, causing her to lose her manuscript. Although she was eventually able to recover a part of it, she was so upset about what had happened that she decided "to take some time off from writing." When she came back to it, she realized her ideas for the book had changed and that she was going to write a different novel from the one she had begun previously. This time it all "came together," and the result is *The Outside World*, another winner.

How many people do you know whose lives were changed for the better when they were compelled to change their plans?

FINAL CONNECTION

Harry Samuels

After submitting the original draft of this manuscript to the publishers, I received a helpful note from their editorial review department. They said the stories were interesting and compelling but needed much help with copy editing. One well-intentioned individual suggested I take a course at a university in creative writing. My response was that at age seventy-three, I was not seeking a Pulitzer Prize; I merely did not wish to be embarrassed. Another suggested I add drama and dialogue to some of the stories, but since they are all true, I felt any additions or changes to the information submitted would not be appropriate. It became apparent I needed some guidance. Two local friends, both accomplished copy editors, offered assistance; however, one could not handle the manuscript for at least six months while the other referred me to someone else.

I was feeling pretty dejected when someone suggested I call Professor Stephen Tabachnick, head of the English Department at the University of Memphis. He gave me the names of two graduate students who might be of help. Before ending our conversation, I mentioned that a number of my anecdotes were heavy in Jewish content. He immediately suggested I speak with Mrs. Jane Lettes, a faculty member in his department. When I spoke with her, she seemed very enthusiastic. She mentioned her husband Arthur had died less than a year earlier, and she felt this project would not only be interesting but therapeutic. She was surprised to learn that her husband and I had been well acquainted and had lunched together perhaps six months prior to his death. Her aunt and uncle were close friends of my aunt and uncle, and they lived next door to each other in an apartment building in Memphis during the 1960s. We also determined that her daughter Jan had traveled with us to Israel in 1976 as part of a family mission. As this book is being written, we are still finding connections with each other.

Those aware of the process that led to our collaboration agree our meeting was truly beshert.

PART VI
BESHERT ROMANCES

5480 2900 0539 8420

02/15/11 03/13
NORMA C SCHLOSSBERG

836-0899

091311

5751981

QUAN.	CLASS	DESCRIPTION				PRICE	AMOUNT
		Beshert / Book					13 95
DATE		AUTHORIZATION	REG./DEPT.	SERVER	CLERK	SUB TOTAL	
REFERENCE NO.						TAX	
FOLIO/CHECK NO.						TIPS/MISC.	

SALES SLIP

TOTAL 13 95

IMPORTANT: RETAIN THIS COPY FOR YOUR RECORDS

CUSTOMER COPY

A SUCCOTH STORY

Rabbi Efraim Greenblatt

When he was approximately nineteen, Rabbi Efraim Greenblatt came to New York from Israel to assist his ailing grandfather in his duties as the rabbi of a Borough Park synagogue. Following the death of his grandfather, he continued to live with his grandmother.

During one Succoth holiday, he and his grandmother decided to visit a nearby community *succah*. It was built to allow observant Jews the opportunity to fulfill the religious injunction of eating within it during that holiday. (Succahs represent the temporary structures built during the forty-year sojourn of the Jews through the desert on their way to the Holy Land.) His grandmother had planned for them to visit one very close to their high-rise apartment, but Rabbi Efraim felt compelled to convince her to travel much farther to another succah. There he noticed a lovely girl and her father who had also come from some distance for the same purpose. Rabbi Greenblatt was attracted to the young lady, but by that time he had been asked to go to Memphis, Tennessee, by his rabbi, the late Rabbi Moishe Feinstein, to serve the Jewish community of that city, and he was not yet ready for serious dating.

Three years later, he again came to visit his grandmother—this time to meet some girls, hoping to find his wife. His grandmother told him she could not understand why he didn't call on a lovely girl she had met whose father was a baker. Rabbi Greenblatt told her he remembered the girl and her father from that meeting three years earlier and said that if she was still as pretty as he had remembered her, he definitely intended to see her. "But tell me how you came to know and appreciate this young lady." She replied that most strangers tended to ignore old ladies they passed on the street. This girl, however, always spoke to her and offered to be of assistance. These simple acts of kindness helped convince her that the girl Miriam was of outstanding character and a fitting wife for her grandson. And so she proved to be, and they were married.

Our city suffered a great loss with the death of Miriam Greenblatt, of blessed memory. She was loved by everyone who knew her. Her many acts of loving-kindness were legendary.

I had planned a book solely of marriages and unusual sequences that played a role in couples' meetings—and I may still write one—but many love stories are also synchronistic and have a place here.

BUCHAREST

Leonid and Friderica Saharovici

Shortly following World War II, Friderica Beck of Bucharest, Romania, graduated from the University of Bucharest with a degree in organic chemistry. She wished to go to another city in order to accept a teaching position; however, under the Communistic regime of the time, she was first required to obtain permission from officials of the Education Department in order to leave the city. She went to the designated office and waited patiently for the official to return. He not only granted her request but told a friend the next day that he believed he was going to marry her.

In 1956, they were married secretly in her mother's bedroom by a rabbi. Even the required witnesses were in attendance in accordance with Jewish law and tradition. Since that atheistic Communist society prohibited such religious ceremonies, it had to be performed clandestinely.

Since coming to our city, the Leonid Saharovicis have become role models of the Memphis community. How fortunate we are that Friderica was required that day to meet her beshert *in a government office of Romania!*

HAUNTING MELODY

Mike Stoller

Mike Stoller was married in 1955. While on their honeymoon, his wife lost her job in Los Angeles, and she was subsequently hired as a bookkeeper and assistant manager of a small jazz record company, Pacific Jazz Records. One of the perks of her new job was the authority to borrow and bring home new releases. Listening to one of those albums one day, Mike heard a singer by the name of Kitty White who was accompanied by Corky Hale on the harp. He says he was smitten by Corky's harp playing as well as the small picture of her on the back of the ten-inch LP record album. But he was married and interested only in Corky's musical talents. (For many years she has been recognized internationally as one of the finest jazz harpists in the world.)

In 1966, the Stollers moved to New York City, and their marriage ended. Mike was living in a hotel that September and asked a date to accompany him to a "happening" at the Armory. Following the program, he was invited to join a group at Sardi's restaurant. He was seated next to a producer who told him of her cute new roommate Corky Hale, a wonderful jazz pianist. An argument then ensued since Mike had remembered her as a harpist, not a pianist. As it turns out, she is outstanding at both, as well as being a singing talent.

Jerry Leiber, Mike's lifelong business partner, dropped by and mentioned that he had recently met Corky in Los Angeles. The next day Jerry invited her to their office in New York to produce some demo recordings, and there she met Mike, to whom she has been very happily married these past thirty-four years.

Mike Stoller and Jerry Leiber are recognized as the "fathers of rock and roll music." They have produced hundreds of songs, including hits by Elvis Presley, Peggy Lee, The Coasters, the Beatles, the Rolling Stones, Barbara Streisand, Frank Sinatra, Sammy Davis, Jr., and more. Their show Smokey Joe's Café *was the longest running musical review in Broadway history. They are still busy composing songs and musical productions, and Corky has added to her many talents by producing television shows and musicals. Mike and Corky are extremely compassionate people. They continue to share their success in numerous ways, benefiting many people who do not even know them.*

MEETING

Alvin and Elaine Gordon

After her graduation from Queens College in New York City, Elaine was seeking a job as a speech therapist. A professor at the college erroneously told one of her classmates that Elaine had been hired by Bellevue Hospital. When the classmate called to congratulate her, Elaine was surprised since she had not applied for the position and was not aware of the opening. That call did induce her to contact Bellevue to see if a position were available. The person who answered her call at Bellevue said the job opening had been filled by someone who had recently worked at the Columbia Presbyterian Hospital. Elaine thanked her and called Columbia Presbyterian, assuming there might now be an opening at that institution. She was correct and was immediately hired for the position that had just been vacated.

Elaine had been working at Columbia Presbyterian for several years when, in July 1959, a co-worker told her that she had two vacation days remaining that were going to expire on July 31. She could not understand why this co-worker kept a record of her vacation days, but since she was an avid tennis player, she decided to use her time for a long weekend at Green Mansions, a tennis resort in the Adirondack Mountains. She asked a girlfriend to accompany her.

Meanwhile, in Memphis, Tennessee, Alvin Gordon, a young single attorney, was invited to the same location. He had repeatedly been invited and had repeatedly rejected the idea of vacationing with his friend Bentley and two others at Green Mansions. That year Bentley persisted and sent the resort a check for Alvin's reservation without telling him. The resort sent Alvin an acknowledgment of his reservation. Although he had never played tennis, Alvin then felt obligated to vacation that year with his persistent friend.

Arriving at Green Mansions, Bentley and two of his friends were housed together, as they usually were each year. Alvin was to share an adjoining cabin with two other men. When he started to unpack, Alvin discovered women's personal effects in his cabin. It seems that Elaine and her friend had been housed there for two days while their accommodations were being repaired. It was understood that the girls would move upon the arrival of the male occupants to whom the cabin had previously been assigned. Elaine met Alvin for the first time when she and her friend returned to see if the new occupants had arrived. That is how Elaine and Alvin began the fulfillment of their synchronistic first meeting, which so far has resulted in forty-three happy years of marriage.

Why do you suppose Elaine's co-worker at Columbia Presbyterian Hospital had tallied her unused vacation time? Recognizing the many achievements of this remarkable couple, that co-worker has had a positive impact on numerous lives in Memphis and around the world.

AFFIRMATION

Harry Samuels

My wife Flora felt compelled to stop playing tennis a few months ago when she began to feel pain in her lower back. The pain seemed to travel to her head. Our immediate concern was to determine if this problem could possibly be connected to an earlier bout with breast cancer (which had been treated successfully). When that scare was ruled out, we checked with an orthopedic surgeon we had met while volunteering at the local Ronald McDonald House. He didn't think it was due to metastasis from her breast cancer but felt a bone scan was in order. The scan confirmed his initial thinking but showed an abnormality in her brain area that was caused by a large, benign meningioma tumor on her brain cover. It was removed successfully last December, and she seems to be well on her way to recovery (thank G-d).

During her recuperation, I soon began experiencing most of her symptoms, including headaches, nausea, sleeplessness, and ear pressure. At first we laughed about it as we recalled her pregnancies when I had experienced morning sickness, though she never did. We also recalled some similar feelings we had long before meeting each other forty-eight years ago.

There is a *midrash,* or legendary story, that sheds some light on these anomalies. According to the story, each soul is composed of both a male and female component, and prior to coming to earth, it divides, with the male portion going into the body of a boy and the female into that of a girl. If the two are truly blessed, their soul is reunited in marriage, a bonding in which they find their soul mate or *beshert.*

Does this suggest another dimension to the term "better half"?

THE WINE CUP

Victor Shine

This is a story of a marriage made in heaven and a wine cup that survived the Holocaust and traveled five thousand miles to my great niece.

Baruch Shine and his brother Victor wanted to attend the wedding of a friend that was being held in Canada, but Baruch's wedding was scheduled a day earlier in Minnesota. Following both weddings, the Shines decided to "crash" the last of the *Sheva Berachot* of their friend. (*Sheva Berachot* are traditionally a week of parties given by family and friends of the newlyweds.) At that party Victor met Chaya (Avner) Engel, the stepmother of the bride. She told him of an outstanding girl, Yona Love, whom she had met years earlier. Chaya subsequently called Yona, who was visiting friends in Israel, to tell her of the terrific fellow she had met. Before Yona could dismiss the idea of getting together with some boy from Memphis, Tennessee, another guest, who was sitting at the same table with her and who overheard part of the conversation, said, "Did you say Victor Shine? He is my good friend and a swell guy. You had better grab him!"

Upon her return to New York, Yona received a call from Victor, and after a five-hour marathon telephone conversation, they decided to meet. Six weeks later they attended a concert held at the Westbury Music Fair in Westbury, New York. During the intermission Victor asked the emcee if he would make the following announcement: "Ladies and gentlemen, before we begin the second half of our show, I have a request from Victor Shine who is seated in section D. 'Yona, will you marry me?'" With a crowd of three thousand yelling encouragement, Yona slumped into her chair mumbling, "Yes." Six months later they were married.

If you are not already convinced that theirs was a marriage made in heaven, read further: The happy couple learned that prior to World War ll, both of their maternal grandmothers had lived in Govorova, a very small town in Poland. Victor's grandmother had given Yona's great, great aunt, Shifra Farber, a tiny silver cup as a wedding present. Shifra had perished in the Holocaust, but the cup was smuggled out of Poland and eventually given to Victor and Yona. They, in turn, presented it to their daughter Shifra, whom they had named after her great, great, great aunt.

Some marriages are truly beshert.

THE BOOK

Henry W. Kimmel

"When I was a teenager, my mother's illness was expected to take her life within six months. Determined, she fought her liver cancer for almost three years—long enough to see me finish high school and almost long enough to see my sister graduate from college.

I wasn't sure what my mother's plans were for my father. They had been married for twenty-five years, and my father seemed worn out from more than two years of seeing to her medical needs. Yet, mother appeared to have a specific plan for him, and to this day I remain overwhelmed by what some may call a coincidence and others may call divine intervention..

Six months after mother died, dad went on a few dates. He didn't want to get involved in a serious relationship, but in his early fifties, he didn't wish to spend his remaining days grieving. John Saladino, an interior designer who had helped my parents plan their new house, arranged a date between my father and Norma Skurka, a fashion reporter for the *New York Times*. John thought my father would enjoy Norma's engaging and spirited personality.

The first date was in my parents' apartment in New York City, and it was going well. The conversation and wine were flowing easily when Norma felt the need to ask a question:

'Are you trying to impress me?' she asked.

'What do you mean?' my father responded.

'That book,' she replied.

'What book?' he asked.

Sitting on the coffee table in front of them was Norma's book, *The New York Times Book of Interior Design and Decorating*. My father had never noticed that book, but my mother had used it diligently in the planning of the new house she had designed but never occupied. Norma and my father thought this was an excellent omen, and they continued to date even during his subsequent illness. When he was given a very short-term prognosis, Norma stood by his side. She helped him with his recovery, one his doctors felt was miraculous. Without

111

Norma, I believe my father would have died. The connection between my mother, Norma's book, and my father's recovery, is something I consider deep and precious. He and Norma were married a few years later, and their union lasted seventeen years, until my father's death in 2002. Norma, my sister, and I still have a bond and loyalty to each other that I wish for all stepparents and stepchildren. Though both of my biological parents are deceased, I feel a strong link for them through Norma and thank G-d for bringing her into our lives in a quirky but seemingly predestined way."

Henry W. (Hank) Kimmel is an accomplished playwrite, attorney, and tennis professional.

PART VII
CHAUTAUQUA

TALES FROM CHAUTAUQUA

Harry Samuels

The Chautauqua Institution, founded in 1874, is situated on beautiful Lake Chautauqua, Chautauqua, New York. It is difficult to describe adequately. It is a magical place filled largely with Victorian homes, cottages and lovely gardens; current issues are presented brilliantly, discussed and debated. There, for nine weeks each summer, thousands come to immerse themselves in cultural, recreational, social, and religious activities. It boasts a magnificent symphony orchestra, live theater, opera, ballet, the longest-running book club in America, and hundreds of other programs for children and adults. Outstanding speakers deliver morning lectures in an amphitheater that often seats 6,500 people. The afternoon lectures are delivered in the "Hall of Philosophy," which is modeled after the Parthenon in Athens, Greece. In that tranquil, tree-studded setting, non-denominational lectures are sponsored five days a week by the Department of Religion. Talks by leading clergy of all religious streams are presented.

We have attended Chautauqua for six years and have made it a part of our lives.

One of the many fascinating experiences we always have there is in meeting such a wide range of interesting people. We often make connections with complete strangers simply by asking the question, "Where are you from?" What can follow never ceases to amaze me!

THE LECTURE

Harry Samuels

Upon our arrival in July 2003, we attended a lecture with approximately 400 others at the Hurlbut Church. It was a slide presentation showing Polish Jewish cemeteries that were desecrated during World War II and the attempts being made to restore them.

We were anxious to start meeting people. Once seated, I turned to my wife and observed that, consistent with our past experiences, we probably had connections with at least half of those present. "Watch this," I remarked, turning to a lady standing before me who was looking toward the rear of the audience prior to the commencement of the program.

"Where are you from?" I asked.

She replied, "I'm from Long Island."

"I've heard of Long Island. That's in the United States, isn't it?" I teased.

"Do you know anyone from Long Island?" she queried.

"Only a couple in Seaford by the name of Geller," I answered. (See "Out of Africa," p.62.)

"They are our best friends," she exclaimed. "We were planning to look you up."

THE WRONG TURN

Philip Pliner

Hearing that I was seeking material for this book, Phillip Pliner, whom we met that same evening, told us about a day he was driving in Queens, New York. For no apparent reason, he took the wrong route over a bridge he had never crossed before. He was attempting to find an explanation for this route when he noticed his daughter standing nearby looking quite distressed. She had just had an automobile accident.

What induced Phil to make a wrong turn that day at that exact time?

A RELATIVE

Harry Samuels

During that week, while waiting for the commencement of a program, I struck up a conversation with a stranger. We sat on one of the benches in the square, had some coffee, and chatted for a few minutes before attending the lecture.

He was born and reared in Oklahoma, and he mentioned that his parents had come to the United States from Eastern Europe early in the last century. They were Jewish, but having witnessed the anti-Semitism and devastation experienced by their relatives during the late 1800s in Europe, they kept a low profile upon immigrating. They did not affiliate with a congregation or make their son aware of their religion. He had grown up attending the Methodist Church and assumed that he was Christian. Since his family never discussed their background, it was only when he entered the U.S. Army during the Korean War that he learned that he was Jewish. Upon receiving his dog tags, he noticed the letters "O" and "H" imprinted. He understood the "O" represented his blood type, but when told the "H" meant that he was Jewish, a fact established by his birth certificate, he found it hard to believe. He spent time with the Jewish chaplain, learning about the faith his parents had attempted to abandon. After much study and soul searching, he embraced the Jewish faith and married a Jewish girl from St. Louis. When I asked her what her maiden name was, I discovered that she was a first cousin of my wife's relative and was also related to my side of the family.

THE PHOTOGRAPH

Harry Samuels

Miriam Fried, the world-famous concert violinist, had just thrilled over six thousand of us in the amphitheater. She played the *Bartok Violin Concerto* to a standing ovation.

Following her performance and the intermission, my wife and I noticed that she had joined her husband, Professor Paul Biss, in the audience.

Professor Biss, too, is an accomplished musician, conductor, and pedagogue, who, like Miriam, teaches at Indiana University's School of Music. Flora and I had met them in Bloomington, Indiana, a few years earlier, so after the performances we stopped to say *hello*. When we finally stood before them, as the crowd began to thin, Professor Biss handed his wife a photograph. He had just received it from an unidentified individual behind the stage. It showed their son Jonathan Biss, the outstanding young concert pianist, and Midori, the violin sensation; it had been taken the previous year when both had performed in the amphitheater at Chautauqua.

Standing beside them in the picture was my wife!

AT THE THEATER

Harry Samuels

It is not so remarkable finding connections with Jewish people in America, especially if one is involved in Jewish charitable organizations, but this one really surprised me.

Waiting in line to enter a theater, my wife and I were introduced to a middle-aged African-American lady. After I asked where she was from (my usual opening upon meeting someone), she replied, "Southern Pennsylvania." I felt sure that my recent streak of making connections was about to end since I knew no one from southern Pennsylvania. During our conversation, the lady alluded to college. When she mentioned "Harvard Law School," I asked if she had ever met my cousin Sarah Sheon who had attended Harvard Law at about that same time.

"Sarah was a year or two ahead of me, but I did know her," she said. "As a matter of fact, I recently saw her deliver some remarks on C-Span." (Sarah Sheon Gerecke has devoted much of her professional life helping to develop low-income housing for the needy of New York City. She is currently the chief operating officer for the Neighborhood Housing Services there.)

When I asked her where she was practicing law, the lady said it was with a firm in Atlanta, Georgia. "Have you ever bumped into my cousin Hersh Bloom, an attorney there? He is related on the other side of my family."

When I mentioned his name, she was very surprised, stating, "He was a former classmate at Harvard and a good friend."

During the performance of the play, I sat next to her and asked if she were ever involved with Leadership Atlanta. When she said that she was a member of that fine group, I asked if she had ever attended the wonderful racial-sensitivity programs that were given to each class.

"Yes, and I will never forget the late Dr. Charles King who directed them. He was also the head of the Urban Crisis Center in Atlanta," she replied. She was surprised to learn that Dr. King and I had been very close. I mentioned that I had offered to accompany him to Memorial Sloan-Kettering Cancer Center at the time of his final illness. He and our son had a special attachment to each other and were great friends. He had given David a book, *Fire In My Bones*, that he had written and inscribed. David insisted it remain beside him during his final illness. The people nearby who observed our conversation were astounded. They began to applaud as they witnessed two apparently unrelated individuals discovering three people in different cities with whom they were both connected.

THE CANTOR

Theo Garb

Theo Garb was seated next to a lady that week in the Hall of Philosophy. Prior to the lecture, they chatted, and he made a remark regarding her British accent. She acknowledged that she had come to the United States after World War II as a war bride from England. "You have a British accent, too," she said. "Where did you acquire yours?"

He told her he was from Dublin, Ireland. "My father served there as a cantor in a large synagogue."

"That's very interesting," she replied. "Many years earlier, I lived on the island of Tortulla. Once I hired a gentleman to conduct the Passover Seder service there for eighty guests. He, too, mentioned that his father had been a cantor in Ireland." The gentleman was Theo's brother.

A FINAL THOUGHT

Harry Samuels

When I showed this manuscript to a good friend, he asserted, "You seem to be suggesting divine intervention in these stories, but we both know you cannot logically prove the existence of a Divine Being." My response to him was that, logically, G-d's existence cannot be proven, but neither can it be disproved by those same syllogistic principles.

There seem to be so many connections and relationships leading us to one another and tying us together. As you have seen, some of them involve the animal world and even metaphysical phenomena. What is the meaning of all this?

Most of these anecdotes had happy endings, yet we know that life can be grim. The person who missed a fatal flight might have made available a seat on that plane for an unfortunate soul. The symphony of life contains both harmony and dissonance.

My purpose in writing this book is not to offer an answer to the questions above, but rather to raise them. It is primarily meant to entertain and to provide examples of unusual situations, experiences and connections that have struck me as interesting and meaningful. I hope you have found these stories interesting, too, and that they will leave you with a greater awareness of the synchronicity in your own life.

WORKS CITED

Dubner, Stephen J. *Turbulent Souls*. New York: W. Morrow, 1998.

Frager, Stanley R. *The Champion Within You: How to Overcome Problems, Obstacles and Adversity in Your Life*. Louisville: Champion, 1992.

King, Charles H. *Fire in My Bones*. Grand Rapids: Wm. B. Eerdmans, 1983.

Mirvis, Tova. *The Ladies Auxilliary*. New York: W.W. Norton, 1999.

—. *The Outside World*. New York: A. Knopf, 2004.

Raz, Simcha. *A Tzaddik In Our Times*. Jerusalem: Feldheim, 1989.

Rigg, Bryan. *Hitler's Jewish Soldiers: The Untold Story of Nazi Racial Laws and Men of Jewish Descent in the German Military*. Lawrence: Kansas UP, 2004.

Secher, Pierre. *Left Behind In Nazi Vienna: Letters of a Jewish Family Caught in the Holocaust 1939-1941*. Jefferson, NC: McFarland, 2004.

Thomas, William H. *Life Worth Living: How Someone You Love Can Still Enjoy Life In a Nursing Home*. Action, MA: VanderWyk and Burnham, 1996.

0-595-31437-6

LaVergne, TN USA
15 March 2011
220079LV00002B/4/A